THE SUPERNATURALIST

A NEW BREED OF BELIEVERS GOVERNED BY THE HOLY SPIRIT

TRACEY ARMSTRONG

T0164486

Cover Design by Allan Nygren
Interior Design by Allan Nygren

ZEBULUN

Published by Zebulun Publishing
www.traceyarmstrong.com

Paperback ISBN 9781952421235

First Edition

Printed in the United States.

TO MY WIFE NATHALIE AND OUR CHILDREN TRISTEN, YOSEF, AND SOPHIA WHO BEAR THE BURDEN AND LEGACY OF BEING A CALLED FAMILY.

TO MY SELFLESS TEAM WHO FIGHT THE GOOD FIGHT OF FAITH ALONGSIDE MY WIFE AND ME FOR A CAUSE THAT IS BIGGER THAN ALL OF US, WHO FIND IT THEIR PRIVILEGE TO PLAY A SMALL PART IN SUCH A LARGE SCHEME.

AND TO AN EMERGING NEW BREED OF CHRIST-FOCUSED "SOLDIERS OF REDEMPTION."

CONTENTS

CHAPTER 1: MY FIRST MIRACLE   1

CHAPTER 2: KNOWING GOD   11

CHAPTER 3: SANCTIFICATION   33

CHAPTER 4: AUTHORITY & POWER   41

CHAPTER 5: THE GIFTS OF REVELATION   55

CHAPTER 6: THE WORD OF WISDOM   71

CHAPTER 7: THE WORD OF KNOWLEDGE   83

CHAPTER 8: DISCERNING OF SPIRITS   93

CHAPTER 9: THE GIFTS OF POWER   105

CHAPTER 10: THE GIFT OF FAITH   113

CHAPTER 11: THE GIFTS OF HEALINGS   123

CHAPTER 12: WORKING OF MIRACLES   135

CHAPTER 13: THE GIFTS OF UTTERANCE   143

CHAPTER 14: PROPHECY   147

CHAPTER 15: DIVERSE KINDS OF TONGUES   165

CHAPTER 16: INTERPRETATION OF TONGUES   171

CHAPTER 17: THE FINAL CALL   177

GIFTS TEST   183

NOTES   185

GIFTS TEST ANSWERS   193

CHAPTER 1

MY FIRST MIRACLE

But one and the same Spirit works all these things, distributing to each one individually as He wills.

1 Corinthians 12:11, NKJV

When I became a Christian, my heart's desire was to do whatever God had need of me to do. My friends and I were accustomed to street evangelism. We would share our testimonies with anyone who would listen, then lead them to the Lord. This is how I spent my first couple weeks as a new believer, scouring the city looking for the lost. When that two-week period ended, I found myself watching a minister on Christian television by the name of Benny Hinn. He was conducting a miracle crusade in Germany. I could hardly believe my eyes. I saw for the first time someone who believed in the power of the Holy Ghost and the fullness of God's Word.

I watched as Benny Hinn prayed for a young girl of about five years old. He stuck his fingers into her ears and said, "In the Name of Jesus, I command these ears to hear and to open." The first time he prayed, seemingly, nothing happened. Then Benny Hinn said, "Everyone, stretch out your hands and pray." After praying again, he tested her hearing by snapping his fingers, checking to see if there was any change in her condition. Immediately the girl responded to a new world of sound. You could see on her face that something was happening through her intense emotional expressions. Indeed, she could hear.

At first, I didn't understand what was going on, other than the obvious that this girl was deaf, but now she could hear. If I had watched an adult being prayed for, I would have dismissed it as fake or some kind of mind control. I didn't believe that a child that young could manufacture such intense emotions. I knew that this was real! I immediately knew in my heart that this favor wasn't only for Benny Hinn but for every man and woman of God who would do whatever the Lord asked of them. In that instance, I prayed, "God, if You can use that man, You can use me."

It's being driven by the love of God for His people that makes us do amazing things for God. When I saw the awe on that young girl's face, I pondered the repercussions of such a miracle in the life of a little child. Think of her friends' responses when they find that she is hearing? Think of the family meeting that needed to happen to explain to the extended family why she can now hear after so many years of deafness. The repercussions of such a dramatic miracle are enormous. This kind of miracle could be the catalyst to whole families coming to the Lord.

I love one-on-one evangelism, but I want to also see families, and possibly communities, swept into the Kingdom of God through this kind of power.

How about you!? Can you imagine the power of God coming through you to change one person's life, causing them to be a catalyst? It's a biblical pattern. When Jesus set the demoniac, living in the tombs, free, Jesus told the man to go preach to the neighboring cities. His miracle became a message of freedom to others. We can empower more people with a message by releasing to them a miracle. We can activate more evangelists by setting them free from the bondage of the enemy.

Think of the effect on a young man or young woman whom you are going to lift from his or her wheelchair in the authority of Jesus. They will never again have to return to a life of bondage and control. Think of the powerful testimony that will be told as a witness of Jesus and His resurrection power. God will empower you to set people free from any bondage and limitations.

When I witnessed that miracle, I didn't realize that the purpose of miracles is to display the resurrection and saving power of Jesus. We must remember that whatever method we use to attract people, that same method will be the only way to keep them. So many are coming to the Lord without being introduced to the supernatural power of God. How can anyone be expected to live above the natural realm if they have never been introduced to the supernatural?

Church services were not to get people saved as much as for equipping the saints for the work of the ministry, which in turn will manifest as believers daily win souls for the Kingdom. In the book of Acts, people came to the church after they were converted in the streets. We must be anointed to take the power of God to the streets where the people are.

Make the next sentence your prayer, "God, if You could use Smith Wigglesworth, John G. Lake, Kathryn Kuhlman, Maria Woodworth-Etter, Benny Hinn, and Billy Graham, you can also use me." God can use you; all you need is faith. Unbelief is the only thing that holds people back from operating in the gifts of God. You and I must have faith that God will use us. If you believe that God can speak to you and that you can hear His voice, you will hear His voice. God speaks to us much more often than we imagine.

Sometimes we may underestimate God's desire to use us. So, when God says, "You can go a mile," we go half a mile; that's where most of us live. When I gave my life to Jesus, I said, "God, I am going to go beyond the limitations of my mind." If God says that you can go two miles, then go two miles; don't allow mediocrity to shortchange you into living below your abilities. So, I stepped out, and I continued stepping out in faith until I saw the results that I desired to see from Him. It was very uncomfortable at first. Success begins when we do whatever it takes, even if it makes us uncomfortable.

We must be prepared to be uncomfortable if we plan to cooperate with the Holy Spirit. The plan of God is not conducive to your comfort zone. One thing that you can always count on is that God is not interested in embarrassing you. Yet, if you desire an amazing life with Him, you cannot live for comfort. I realized this years later while sitting under Lester Sumrall's ministry. The day I waged war on leisure. I will share more about that in a later chapter.

God is more interested in using you than embarrassing you. He will never cause you to be put to shame, but He will always encourage you to go beyond your own limitations. Sin introduced mankind to limitation through the fall of man in the garden. There was no limitation until there was disobedience. Obedience produces "possibility living," and disobedience produces limitation in life. We have to step out of our comfort zone to touch people who are uncomfortable through life's trials. When we embrace this kind of obedience, we will recognize that it's really a life of faith. God has removed the ceiling from our limitation and we can now grow in Him as much as we desire.

GOD GIVES WHAT HE HAS PROMISED

The ultimate goal of Jesus wasn't to show off how much power He possessed. His coming was to be an example to us of what we can become and do for the Kingdom of God if we surrender to Him. He revealed the pattern in which we should walk and live every day. Jesus lived life to the fullest and so should we, going about doing good, casting out demons, healing all who are oppressed of the devil, and living our lives to win souls. I must add, as a side note, that He did this while leading an organization with twelve executives. When we read the book of John, we shouldn't pattern our lives after John or Peter, but we should walk in a pattern that is fashioned after Jesus' image. God did not put a carrot on a string and a stick, saying to us, "Come on get the carrot," and every time we reach for it, He yanks it back and says, "Sorry, you can't have this." That would be false advertising. Jesus is the perfect image of what a surrendered and submitted man or woman looks like. And God gave Him as an achievable pattern.

Have you ever gone to a fast-food restaurant, and while you were looking at the menu, you see a picture of a juicy, delicious looking burger? The cheese is perfectly melted, with lettuce, onion, and tomato. Quickly, you order the triple deluxe double burger. Your mouth is watering, your taste buds are dancing, and your stomach is humming. With great expectation, you open the lid, and to your amazement, you find a disaster in a box. The wilted lettuce has slipped off the burger and it is lying on the side, the cheese is not melted, and the patty feels like it's been in the refrigerator all morning. That's not like our God. He gives what He promises.

If you run hard after God, He will reward you with what you are running after. Running hard after God is not an easy way of life, it is a challenging way of life. Yet, it is a rewarding and adventurous way of life. In truth, it should be our only way of life.

When I got saved and set free from drugs, the first thing that I did was make my bedroom into a sanctuary. The book of Acts became very real to me the more I read about the miraculous things that were happening in the early church. I noticed in the book of Acts that the supernatural acts were just as evident on a daily basis outside of the four walls of the church as within the walls of the church. As the disciples went about their daily lives, miracles happened. They didn't set up special outreach moments. Their lives were the outreach moment. I soon started preaching on the street corners and on public buses, talking to everyone who would listen, and bothering everyone who wouldn't. When I couldn't find someone to preach to, I preached to my dresser and my bedpost. I was a preaching machine. I got a lot of "no thanks" responses in those days, while trying to minister on the streets, but that didn't bother me. I was zealous, so I didn't mind the nos. I just figured that most people didn't understand what they were missing. I had discovered the most powerful relationship that I had ever experienced. I was not ashamed of what I knew about Christ. In my mind, everyone needed to be made aware of Him the way that I had been enlightened. This is still my belief: all must know Jesus as their Lord and Savior.

No matter how many times you get rejected, never give up. Rejection is never easy, yet rejection should never be allowed to cripple your faith. As I walked around, I would pray, "I am going to keep doing this until You show up." In the Bible, a woman persistently approached a judge for help until he answered her petition. After a while, the Judge got so tired of hearing from her that he decided to fulfill her request. This same thing will happen for you and me when we approach God persistently, asking the Lord for His involvement in our lives.

I JUST CAN'T STOP

After riding the bus and having very few results, I would go back to my bedroom to complain to God about lacking the power to change lives. I reminded God of His Word as Moses did, saying, "God, You promised that signs would follow Your Word, and I see this in the book of Acts. I committed my life to the God of the Bible. You must be that God, or else I will go out and find Him. If You cannot do what this book says, then You're a liar, and I am not willing to serve a liar." I was a foolish young man to talk to God that way. Yet, I still find that same radical conviction in my heart today. I often find myself having very real conversations like this with God. Then, I didn't know to beware. I was so sick of living a mediocre life and I needed Jesus to be real. I didn't know what else to do with my life. My goal was not to prove God wrong; my hope was that God would prove me wrong. I think that there are a lot of young people who want to know that God is real. This generation is not looking for another powerless and religious Christian service; they want the real thing. This generation has the spirit of Elisha. They are crying out asking, "Where is the God of Elijah?" They are ready to be equipped and mobilized into the harvest.

I don't think God approved of everything that I said and did, but I do think He liked my heart and my determination. My mind was made up. It didn't matter to me how many people I had to preach to or pray for, somebody was going to get saved, healed, or delivered. Their life would never be the same. If one person gets touched or saved, I thought, it won't matter how many people said no. The price has been paid for a life to be changed. It is worth all of the persecution, all of the spitting, and all the different things that you will undoubtedly experience to reach that one soul.

I remember one time when I drove up to Seattle to witness, I preached on a concrete structure across the street from Westlake Center. As I finished preaching, I walked down to hand out tracts to people who were walking by. As I stretched out my hand to give a tract to a man passing by, this gentleman started using all types of obscenities. As if that wasn't enough, I looked up to see his lips forming into a spout for saliva. Suddenly, a putrid rocket of saliva left his mouth and headed toward my face. All I could think was, *please don't land on my face.* By the mercies of God, the drop of rejection missed my face and landed on my chest.

You have to be ready for anything. If you call yourself a Christian and you do not think that persecution is going to come, then you're fooling yourself. You're right where the devil wants you. Jesus was persecuted and so will His followers be persecuted. People may even call you a fanatic. Yes, you may experience resistance. Even though some will reject your message, the ready ones will openly receive it. I remember when I started laying hands on people and they started getting touched by the power of God. Christian people immediately came and told me that I couldn't be used in that way because I was too young. Some even said, "God doesn't do that anymore." Another told me that if I expected God to move in my meetings and Bible studies supernaturally, I was putting God into a box. To say that God can or cannot do something is putting God into a box. How can we, the dust of the earth, tell the Creator of the universe what He can or cannot do?

Go to the Word when this happens. It will save you a lot of trouble. If you understand what God says, then you will be able to stand and make it through any rejection. Because of these opposing voices, it took me a while to believe God completely at His word. I let the words and accusations from people who didn't have the power of God in their own lives stop me from stepping out in faith. Do not allow anyone to put limitations on your ability to grow and develop in God. If it is the will of God and if it is scriptural, you just keep on doing it. Protect your relationship with God, love His people, and win the lost.

THE GIFTS

There are three categories of gifts: The Gifts of Revelation, The Gifts of Power, and The Gifts of Utterance. The Gifts of Revelation include the Word of Wisdom, the Word of Knowledge, and Discerning of Spirits. The Gifts of Power include the Gift of Faith, the Gift of Healings, and the Workings of Miracles. The Gifts of Utterance include the Gift of Prophesy, the Gift of Tongues, and the Gift of Interpretation of Tongues.

It is important to understand that the Holy Spirit works differently with each individual. Some of the ways that He uses me may be different from the way that He chooses to use you. The way that you partner with Him will depend a great deal on your personality and calling. I pray that as you read this book, your desire to win souls and to know God will increase as you learn to walk with the Holy Spirit. I pray that as you read this book, you will find a relationship with the Holy Spirit that you never had before, resulting in new excitement and enthusiasm for ministering to others. The gifts of the Spirit are graces that God has given to us so that we can be His witnesses to the un-churched, as well as bring restoration to the churched. The gifts will become some of your greatest assets for winning souls. The Holy Spirit will teach you and lead you daily in your personal life. If one thing from this book can help you to help someone else, it is all worth it. There are no formulas for getting the Holy Spirit to operate with you; all you need is faith, trust, and availability. If you have a little bit of faith, if the Holy Spirit can trust you, and if you are available at any moment, then look forward to some awesome adventures in God. Enjoy the journey!

CHAPTER 2

KNOWING GOD

But the people that do know their God shall be strong, and do exploits.

...the people who know their God shall be strong, and carry out [great exploits.]

Daniel 11:32, NKJV

You must know God before you can introduce anyone else to Him. It is not enough to know *about* God, but you must truly know Him. In most cultures and religions, there is a pursuit to know God; to know His thoughts, feelings, intentions, and plans. In Christianity, this pursuit is a way of life. In the laws of Moses, God made Himself known through His many names. Jehovah means self-existent, eternal, or Lord. Many times you will find added to His name Jehovah, attributes that describe God's character, such as Jehovah-Jireh, which means "Lord God, my provider," or more accurately, "the God who sees." In another place, He is called Jehovah-Rapha, which means "Lord God, my healer." The names of God are not meant to label nor identify God as much as they are synonymous with His presence, His divine manifestation, and His nature.

EXPERIENCING GOD

It is also possible to know God through what we have experienced of Him: by what we have seen, heard, and handled. The Hebrew word for this type of knowing is *yada*, to know by experience, to know (a person carnally), or to be known. Daniel 11:32 (KJV) says, "But the people that do know their God shall be strong, and do exploits." The people who have experiential knowledge of their God shall be strong and take action.

We are empowered to manifest God as we grow in our knowledge of Him. We must take note of Exodus 6:3 (NASB), "I appeared to Abraham, Isaac, and Jacob, as God Almighty, but *by* My name, LORD, I did not make Myself known to them." Moses' initial encounter with God was based upon the already familiar knowledge of God. Yet, Moses wanted more. Moses was the first to ask for and to receive the name of God. When the Lord appeared to Moses, He introduced Himself as the God of Abraham, Isaac, and Jacob. Moses wasn't satisfied with this introduction. The patriarchs were chosen to receive the promise and God was ready to fulfill His Word; therefore, He chose Moses as His deliverer. In Genesis 3, Moses asked the Lord, "Who should I say sent me, in whose name do I go?" (Genesis 3:13 paraphrase). The Lord replies, "I AM WHO I AM" (Genesis 3:14) this means, "I Exist who Exist." Morris Cerullo said that every assignment anointing of God is presented by an encounter. You and I cannot do what has never been done unless we have an encounter with God that we have never had before. Only then can we carry a level of God and manifest the higher nature associated with His name.

IN THE NAME OF JESUS

In whose name will you go? You cannot go in the name of the God of Smith Wigglesworth, Kathryn Kuhlman, John G. Lake, or even Paul the Apostle. You must be prepared to go in the name of the God who you know, in the name of Jesus. We have people trying to do things in the name of another person's god. We must remind ourselves of the tragic outcome of the seven sons of Sceva (Acts 19:11-17).

We must be able to preach, pray, prophesy, and prosper in the name of Jesus. When we can do this from the heart, and with the confidence of the Lord, then will our names be on the most honored list in Hell. We will be named among the mighty, and our names will be listed on the "Paul I know, and Jesus I know" fear list in hell. If this list isn't familiar, take a moment and read Acts 19:15, and you will recognize the reference.

God is interested in revealing Himself to us in an intimate way. Intimacy does not just mean knowing God, but also being known by God. The Bible says that God knows those who are His. Abraham, Isaac, and Jacob knew (yada) God as almighty, and because of their knowledge of the Almighty, they were able to trust Him for the promises that He made to them. When the Lord revealed Himself to Moses, it revolutionized the way that all mankind would communicate with and relate to God. From that point on, man became an instrument of God's utterance and miracle-working power.

It would be criminal for us to experience God's heart and not be able to distribute His goodness and amazing glory. It would be tormenting. Imagine God reveals to you that He wants to deliver the children of Israel out of the hand of the Egyptians, but He withholds from you the power to set them free. Any involvement would be fulfilling, whether uttering a promise or displaying His miracle-working power to deliver them. Revelation of a problem is worthless without the promise of hope or the power to rectify the problem. On the same note, the power of miracles and prophetic utterance are destructive without the heart of God.

When we seek to know God, our hearts become entangled with His. The result is us falling in love with Him and the things that are important to Him. Moses' relationship with God instantly changed when he encountered Him. God not only appeared to Moses and spoke to him, but the Lord also worked miracles through him. This was something that the children of Israel had never experienced. The time that Moses spent with the Lord shifted from communication into communion.

COMMUNION

Communion turns into love, and love is the motivation of God. It's not enough to only know God as Creator. It's not enough to know Him as Savior. We must make Him Lord and seek to know Him as Lord.

> And whatever you ask in My name, that I will do, that the Father may be glorified in the Son. If you ask anything in My name, I will do *it*. If you love Me, keep My commandments.
>
> John 14:13-15, NKJV

The word love, in verse 15, is the word *agapao* (ag-ap-a"-o) in Greek, which means to love in a social or a moral sense. To love in a social sense is to seek out and enjoy the company of someone: it's companionship. If you truly desire to know Jesus, you must seek Him with all your heart.

SOCIAL LOVE

Although I love my wife more than any other person in the world, if I had to choose whether to spend time with Jesus or my wife, Jesus would be my choice. Our love for God should take precedence over everything else.

I often feel a strong presence of God come upon me in what we would normally consider inopportune times, like when I am eating, watching a movie, or spending time with friends. It is vitally important to obey when you feel the leading of the Lord. The Holy Spirit often reveals Himself to us for the sake of ministry. You and I must become familiar with being led by the Spirit. The Bible states that those who are led by the Spirit are the Sons of God (see Romans 8:14). Most believers never develop the sensitivity to the presence of God to know His actions. It is a small thing to abandon everything to fellowship with the almighty God. I challenge you to seek enjoyment from His company and watch what happens as the Holy Spirit trusts you to respond to His leading.

MORAL LOVE

Moral love means that you would never consciously do anything that would damage your relationship with the one whom you love. There are many who tell God that they love Him but turn their backs on Him when He calls to meet with them. Love will never purposely hurt, manipulate, or grieve the one whom it loves. The Holy Spirit is drawing us into a deeper realm of intimacy with Him, which will result in Him giving us greater revelation and responsibility.

Agapao, which means love, describes a willingness to do anything and everything to be with the one that it loves, and do nothing to offend the one that it loves. John 14:15 says, "If you love Me, keep My commandments." I believe that the phrase, "keep My commandments," doesn't just mean to keep the laws or statutes of God. The word commandment is the Greek word *entol* (en-tol-a"), which means an "authoritative prescription." When we go to the doctor, we expect the doctor to be an authority on the human body. With this expectation, we trust that he will give us the proper prescription to aid in healing our body. God is the authority on life, and when we abandon all to be in His presence, He too will give us His authoritative prescriptions for dealing with any need or circumstance that may arise.

> If you love Me, keep My commandments. And I will
> pray the Father, and He will give you another Helper,
> that He may abide with you forever.
>
> John 14:15-16, NKJV

Verse 16 speaks of another comforter, helper, or in Greek, *parakletos* (par-ak'-lay-tos), which is an intercessor, counselor, or stand by. If the King James translators had translated this verse with the understanding that it is supposed to convey, it would read differently in my observation.

If you seek Me with all of your heart, abandoning all to be with Me, doing nothing to hurt or grieve Me, the Holy Spirit, your helper and teacher, will speak to you My authoritative prescriptions. And I will pray to My Father and He will send the Holy Spirit to be someone who will stand by you, to celebrate when you want to celebrate, to teach you, to guide you, to lead you, and to remind you of the image and likeness you were created after. TAI (Tracey Armstrong Interpretation)

I get so excited as I think of that very long yet true description of the perfect relationship with the Holy Spirit. This is the perfect foundation for understanding how Jesus functioned in revelation and power.

SEE AND HEAR

Jesus gives two keys to the secret of His supernatural lifestyle in John 5:19 and 30. The first is that He only did what He saw the Father do.

> Then Jesus answered and said to them, "Most assuredly,
> I say to you, the Son can do nothing of Himself, but what

He sees the Father do; for whatever He does, the Son
also does in like manner."

John 5:19, NKJV

When we put our visions and self-determined purposes to the side,
allowing the vision and prophetic revelation of the Father to manifest
in our hearts, we will be led by the Spirit and not by the flesh. You and
I will fulfill the desires of the Father and accomplish the will of God as
people who are totally surrendered to the Holy Spirit.

The second key is that Jesus' ears were attentive to the voice of the
Father, always listening for the sweetness of His Father's guiding voice.
Jesus, in His humanity, realized that His decision-making ability was
limited, stating:

I can of mine own self do nothing: as I hear, I judge: and
my judgment is just; because I seek not mine own will,
but the will of the Father which hath sent me.

John 5:30, KJV

When we cast away our personal agendas to take on the mantle and
Christlikeness of our Lord, abandoning all foolishness for the perfect
will of God, we will do as Jesus did: see what the Father is doing and do
just the same. We will hear the voice of the Father and judge correctly.

When we live as "supernaturalists," we will walk as our perfect example walked. Not just living a natural or normal life because we as humans
have limitations, but living supernatural lives as we serve in a supernatural kingdom: seeing, listening, handling, and experiencing the supernatural things of God. For this reason, the Holy Spirit is with us to abide
with us forever, to help us live as supernaturalists, and to destroy the
works of the devil.

I have yet many things to say unto you, but ye cannot bear them now. Howbeit when he, the Spirit of truth, is come, he will guide you into all truth: for he shall not speak of himself; but whatsoever he shall hear, that shall he speak: and he will shew you things to come. He shall glorify me: for he shall receive of mine, and shall shew it unto you. All things that the Father hath are mine: therefore said I, that he shall take of mine, and shall shew it unto you.

John 16:12-15, KJV

Many believe that God is finished showing revelation and speaking to His people, but Jesus spoke just the opposite. Jesus said that the Spirit is going to be with us forever, even unto the end of the world. The Holy Spirit is actively transforming us into the very image and likeness of Christ through revelation and the power of God.

I WANT TO KNOW YOU MORE

One day, I asked the Father how I could know Him in a greater way. He said that if I would pay the price and spend time with the Holy Spirit, the Holy Spirit would help me know Jesus in a greater way. And once I knew Jesus, then I would know the Father. As the scripture says, the Holy Spirit will never speak of Himself; His purpose is to glorify Jesus.

The grace of the Lord Jesus Christ, and the love of God, and the communion of the Holy Ghost, be with you all. Amen.

2 Corinthians 13:14, KJV

Our communion with the Holy Ghost leads us into greater under-standing of the other two persons of the Godhead. At one point, I decided to schedule a time daily to meet with the Holy Spirit for half an hour. This time was not to include intercession, worship, reading, petition, suppli-cation, or thanksgiving. This time was only for communion; just to see and listen. I found a private place where I would not be interrupted and set the time for 6:00 p.m. every day. When I entered the room, I would lock the door behind me and only speak five words for the whole thirty minutes: "Holy Spirit, I am here." The first few times I didn't see, hear, or feel anything or anybody. Around the third or fourth day, He came in a tangible way. In such a way that it felt as if I was standing in the middle of a room filled with gelatin. Although everything inside of me wanted to scream and shout with joy, I continued in silence. I started with my hands stretched forth to Heaven, but as the atmosphere filled with the glory of God, I was forced to sit. He began to speak of things to come, things that He desired to do in the city in which I was living. He spoke to me about my immediate family as well as my future family, as I was single at the time.

Day after day, we met. At first, it would take a few minutes for me to realize that He was there. After a while, I couldn't even finish saying, "Holy Spirit, I am here," before His presence filled the room. Until this very day, I have these intimate times with the Holy Spirit, but most of the time it is spontaneous. Sometimes He wakes me up in the middle of the night and shares secrets with me. I feel as if we truly walk together on a daily basis, and this all started with setting apart some time to listen for the voice of the Spirit. If we would slow down, shut the world out, and listen, the Holy Spirit would talk to us regarding the things that He has seen and heard from Jesus.

THE TEACHER

As a result, my understanding of the Word of God increased. After all, I was meeting with the author of the Bible! If you desire to have a greater revelation of the Word, just talk to the author, He's eager to teach us. At times, I could sense that He was more excited to teach me than I was to learn. The most important thing for a teacher is to have a student who is eager to learn.

The more time I spent with Him, the more passionate I became. My prayer life took off. I became increasingly curious about the things of the Kingdom of God and started asking the Holy Spirit to reveal to me the secrets of the Kingdom.

The Holy Spirit began to give me the desires of my heart. Meaning, God's desires became my desires. In order to know God, we must commune with the Holy Spirit. He is our teacher, and only He can bring to our attention the things that are important to the Father. Only He can bring to our remembrance all the things that Jesus spoke. The communion that we are discussing here is called, *koinonia* (koy-nohn-ee'-ah); partnership, (social) intercourse, communication, communion, or fellowship. This word describes an intellectual interchange. Communication with the Godhead is the ultimate goal. We desperately need to have a conversation with the Holy Spirit to gain insight from each person of the Godhead, through the help of the Holy Spirit. The Holy Spirit draws us closer to Jesus who, in turn, shows us the Father. Our communication and social interaction with the Holy Spirit causes us to understand the grace of Jesus, without which we could never understand the love of the Father.

> Jesus saith unto him, I am the way, the truth, and the life: no man cometh unto the Father, but by me. If ye

had known me, ye should have known my Father also: and from henceforth ye know him, and have seen him. Philip saith unto him, Lord, show us the Father, and it sufficeth us. Jesus saith unto him, Have I been so long time with you, and yet hast thou not known me, Philip? He that hath seen me hath seen the Father; and how sayest thou then, Show us the Father?

John 14:6-9, KJV

In verses 6 and 7, we get a better understanding of Jesus' desire for us to know Him and the Father. "If you know me, then you know the Father." I must go on to say that since we didn't walk in the flesh with Jesus, the only way for us to know Christ is our communication with Him through His words and the Holy Spirit.

That which was from the beginning, which we have heard, which we have seen with our eyes, which we have looked upon, and our hands have handled, of the Word of life; (For the life was manifested, and we have seen it, and bear witness, and shew unto you that eternal life, which was with the Father, and was manifested unto us;) That which we have seen and heard declare we unto you, that ye also may have fellowship with us: and truly our fellowship is with the Father, and with his Son Jesus Christ.

I John 1:1-3, KJV

Earlier in this chapter, we discovered that the Hebrew word *yada* means to know by seeing, hearing, or experiencing. Verse 1 gives us the understanding that the disciples (at least John) knew Jesus through experience and not merely through rumor or studious knowledge.

When Nathalie and I first met, my interest in her was so strong that I had no reservation about driving two hours round trip to spend sometimes as little as forty minutes with her. I oftentimes would call one of my friends just so that I could talk about Nathalie, who is now my wife. It seemed that every conversation turned into a time of praise about Nathalie. I am sure that my friends were tired of hearing about her, but that didn't matter to me because I couldn't get enough of talking about her. The more time that I spent with her, the more I would have to say. My communion with her took control of my conversations.

LOSING CONTROL

In the same way, our communion with God will take control of our conversations. As we commune with the Holy Spirit, we can experience Jesus. The Holy Spirit loves revealing Jesus to us. So much so that all He truly desires to talk about is Jesus: what Jesus said and did for us, to us, and what He desires to do through us. As we become closer to Jesus, He truly loves to show us the Father, who first loved us enough to give us grace through Jesus, His son.

Our lives will influence people because of what the Holy Spirit is showing us about the fullness of the Godhead during our times of communion with Him. It will cause people to be drawn into this same fellowship (koinonia) with the Father, Son, and the Holy Spirit.

This is the secret to walking in the realms of the supernatural! We are influenced by who we associate with. It takes no effort to maintain a dead spiritual lifestyle, but if you desire more than what you have now, it will take doing something that you have not done before. The truth is that doing something new may be uncomfortable at first, but it will be extremely rewarding in the end. If we will pay the price to be in the presence of the Lord, then we will be transformed into His image. What a glorious possibility!

SHOCKED BY THE BOLDNESS

Peter and John, on their way to the temple at the hour of prayer, ran across a beggar at the entrance of the temple. They were drawn to this man crying for their assistance and were compelled to help. Love and compassion are the only forces that can compel us to help others. Peter, fixing his eyes on the man, said to him, "I do not have silver and gold, but what I do have I give to you: In the name of Jesus Christ the Nazarene, walk!" (Acts 3:6, NASB). Peter wasted no time on doubt and unbelief; he grabbed the man by the hand and pulled him to his feet. The man received his miracle! This opened a door for them to share the Gospel with all who knew the man who now was healed. While they were still sharing the good news, the temple guards seized Peter and John to deliver them to the religious leaders. While under their interrogation, Peter, filled with the Holy Spirit, began to rebuke the religious leaders. They were so shocked by the boldness and confidence of Peter and John, and with the miracle that was performed, that they were speechless.

> Now when they saw the boldness of Peter and John, and perceived that they were uneducated and untrained men, they marveled. And they realized that they had been with Jesus. And seeing the man who had been healed standing with them, they could say nothing against it.
>
> Acts 4:13-14, NKJV

Imagine how these leaders felt as they looked upon Peter and John and realized that there was something familiar about these men. They considered their credentials and found that they were not students of the Law. They wondered how these men could speak with such boldness; how these unpolished and unrefined men could be used by God. It was so shocking to their traditional standards that they were speechless. They could say nothing to refute the miracle. The boldness of these two men seemed familiar, but they couldn't pinpoint the source. I can imagine that each time Peter spoke, they would see a face flash before their eyes, the face of Jesus. They saw the same conviction of heart that Jesus had. They reasoned among themselves and could only credit this boldness to the communion that they had with Jesus. While they were with Him, the passion of Jesus burned into their souls to the point that the scholars saw the resemblance.

Scripture says that we all, with unveiled faces, behold in a mirror the glory of God (see 2 Corinthians 3:18). You are what you look at; it will surely reflect in your life. The grace of God's image should be on your heart and manifest in your life. We can all experience this transformation of soul and spirit when we commune with the Lord. His glory is going to burn so deep into us that our faces will shine, our lips will reveal the secrets of God, and our lives will be a divine connection between Heaven and Earth. Imagine the endless adventures we have ahead of us as we press toward the mark of the high calling to be transformed into the image of God Almighty.

We must realize that Jesus didn't simply come to die so that we could be saved from the damnation of eternal hell, but He also came to set the stage for world dominion and individual transformation. Christ is the mold for our transformation; Christ is the pattern for our lives, and through us, He will establish the heavenly destiny of God in the earth.

People will be drawn through the love of God that resides within us. They will draw on the glory within, just as the woman with the issue of blood did with Jesus. May the hurting people of the world be able to draw the virtue of God from the depth of your being and find help from God! The deeds of God will follow you: soul winning, deliverance, and healing through God's supernatural ability will be a daily and vital part of your life. Boldness will overpower you and will cause you to do outrageous things for the Kingdom of God. You will fall so in love with the Lord that your heart will leap when you hear His voice, and you will be compelled to share everything that you know about Him. This is what happened to Peter and John. After the miracle and the confrontation with Pharisees, the religious leaders rebuked them and told them not to preach in the name of Jesus.

> But Peter and John answered and said to them, "Whether it is right in the sight of God to listen to you more than to God, you judge. For we cannot but speak the things which we have seen and heard."
>
> Acts 4:19-20, NKJV

When we are in the presence of the Holy Spirit, we are drawn closer to Jesus, and as we grow closer to Jesus, the Father is revealed to us. All along, the Holy Spirit is showing us things to come and speaking to us the authoritative prescription of the Lord. This is where we find our identity, which is based upon our seat or throne in heavenly places. The Holy Spirit will teach you and encourage you until you are free from your limitations. His words will come to you and me through what we have seen in visions, dreams, spiritual revelation, and natural and spiritual experiences. You will also speak of the things that you have heard from the Throne Room regarding the Kingdom. The Holy Spirit will reveal to us the schemes of the enemy, as well as bring prophetic edification, exhortation, comfort, and foresight of things to come.

AS THE SPIRIT WILLS

The Holy Spirit is the one who manifests what God the Father wants in the earth. The greater your reliance on the Holy Spirit, the easier it will be for you to win the lost and help hurting people. The Holy Spirit delivers the gifts according to His will, as Jesus determined, as the Father desires.

> For to one is given the word of wisdom through the Spirit, to another the word of knowledge through the same Spirit, to another faith by the same Spirit, to another gifts of healings by the same Spirit, to another the working of miracles, to another prophecy, to another discerning of spirits, to another *different* kinds of tongues, to another the interpretation of tongues. But one and the same Spirit works all these things, distributing to each one individually as He wills.
>
> 1 Corinthians 12:8-11, NKJV

We have been misled to believe that we can use the gifts whenever, however, and for whatever reason we want. God divides to us the gifts of the Spirit as He determines, for the reason He determines. The Holy Spirit gives us the gifts according to our desire, with one aim in mind: to reach the lost, and to equip the saints for the work of ministry.

The gifts of the Spirit will operate fully in connection with our personality and our strengths. Paul talked about coveting the different gifts. The gifts of the Holy Spirit cannot be used without the Holy Spirit's involvement. The Holy Spirit delivers gifts to us, and we use His gifts for His will and for His glory. The truth is not that man uses the gifts of the Holy Spirit, but rather the Holy Spirit, who occupies man and fills him, uses that person and manifests the gifts through him according to His own will, time, and situation.

The Holy Spirit is distributing the gifts to individuals as He wills. God desires for every person to receive at least one of the gifts of the Spirit. It makes no difference what denomination you are involved with; the Holy Spirit has no dispensational limitations and denominational barriers.

> God also bearing witness both with signs and wonders, with various miracles, and gifts of the Holy Spirit, according to His own will?
>
> Hebrews 2:4, NKJV

The gifts of God are for the sole purpose of testifying of the resurrection of Jesus. The gospel is God's power unto salvation, and if we are to preach the good news, we must preach it with the power of the Holy Spirit, displaying to the world the resurrection power of the Spirit. The gospel is not to be shared with only influential speech, but with demonstration.

Wrong teaching instructs that the gifts of God are dead. If the gifts are dead, then the Holy Spirit has left the earth. As long as He is here, His communication and manifestation are here. Dispensationalists will tell you that we have matured beyond the gifts. If that were true, we would be sitting across the table from Jesus and the world would be saved.

Don't be ignorant, we have much work to do, and we are going to need the Holy Spirit to get the job done. As pastors and ministers, we must stop thinking that we can lead our churches and ministries into the greatest and most powerful season the church has ever experienced on our own. If the glory of the latter house is to be greater than the former house, we must stop throwing away the foundations that were laid by previous generations and start building on them. We can tell if the Holy Spirit has control of a life or a church by what is being followed.

Is the Holy Spirit bearing witness in your life? The devil hates the man or woman who allows the Holy Spirit to bear witness in his or her life.

In these last days, the devil is opening his arsenal. False teachers, false prophets, and false miracles are seen left and right. God is looking for soldiers who will rise up in the pure gifts of God that will confound the wise. We can't allow the devil to get an upper hand by drawing the world to his false, deceiving manifestations of power. The staff of God will consume the staff of Pharaoh. Could you imagine if God had sent Moses to Pharaoh without the power to back up the word of the Lord? He would have been laughed out of the palace. The children of Israel would have stayed in Egypt. Just as Moses was empowered for his generation, Peter and Paul for their generation, we are anointed and empowered for this present time and generation.

BEWARE OF RELIGIOUS REPETITION

All we need to do is submit to the Holy Spirit and allow Him to use us as He wills. Give God the permission to interrupt us while we are in the grocery store line paying for our groceries. Be ready to minister to the person behind the counter who has problems in his or her marriage. We need to listen for the still small voice as He whispers, "That man has a problem in his life, and I want you to give him a message." Quickly and directly, respond by asking the person behind the counter, "May I encourage you with a few things?" Share what God has said and that person's life could be dramatically changed. As you walk off, that person will realize how much God must love them to have sent you to the grocery store with a message just for them. The Lord will give you a word of knowledge or a prophetic word to help someone in need. He will give you insightful words of wisdom, discernment of spirits, or something that will help them through their toughest time or get their attention so that they are ready to hear the gospel.

In the early ministry of Moses, we saw him with God interceding for mercy for the people, communing with God, and asking for advice on how to lead God's people. But after being in the wilderness with the children of Israel for a while, Moses' heart grew cold towards them, the same people that he, at one time, would have died for. Since they continued to go around in circles, they found themselves again in the same place where there had been a drought. The first time the people murmured, Moses pleaded on behalf of the people to God, asking God to supply their need with fresh drinking water. The Lord commanded Moses to strike the rock with his rod. The rod is a symbol of the gift of God. It was one of the things that the Lord gave to Moses as a sign to the children of Israel and Pharaoh that God was with him to deliver the children of Israel from Egypt.

For this same reason, God has given us gifts of the Holy Spirit so that all will know that God is with us. Moses took his rod, struck the rock, and suddenly water gushed out of the rock to meet the needs of the people. Moses was able to manifest water for the people from the rock by being led by the Holy Spirit. Some are hitting the rock without the leading of the Holy Spirit, meaning they do not fully rely on God and His power. It is easy to get too familiar with being used by God. Eventually, we find more formulated ways to create the appearance of the unction of God. Humanity is resourceful, we have created systems and processes to grow just about everything except for deep intimacy with the living God. I believe that everything we do for God and His Kingdom must be world-class and excellent, but that can never replace intimacy and the anointing of God. We may strike the rock without the instruction of the Holy Spirit, and God, by His great mercy, will still minister the water from the rock to His people. He did it for Moses, but not without Moses losing something in return. There will always be a price for disobedience.

The second time around in this land of Zin, the people of Israel continued in their old ways. They chose the bondage of Egypt over the place that God was leading them through.

> So Moses and Aaron went from the presence of the assembly to the door of the tabernacle of meeting, and they fell on their faces. And the glory of the LORD appeared to them. Then the LORD spoke to Moses, saying, "Take the rod; you and your brother Aaron gather the congregation together. Speak to the rock before their eyes, and it will yield its water; thus you shall bring water for them out of the rock, and give drink to the congregation and their animals." So Moses took the rod from before the LORD as He commanded him. And Moses and Aaron gathered the assembly together before the rock; and he said to them, "Hear now, you rebels! Must we bring water for you out of this rock?" Then Moses lifted his hand and struck the rock twice with his rod; and water came out abundantly, and the congregation and their animals drank. Then the LORD spoke to Moses and Aaron, "Because you did not believe Me, to hallow Me in the eyes of the children of Israel, therefore you shall not bring this assembly into the land which I have given them."
>
> Numbers 20:6-12, NKJV

MERCY MINISTRY

Moses was so aggravated with these people that he spoke to them instead of to the rock in front of him. This was his first mistake; he let his heart grow cold towards the people that he had to serve. Pass this test and you will last until we go to Heaven. God wanted to give them a new level of faith as they watched Moses speaking to the rock instead of hitting the rock. Moses gave in to a fit of rage and struck the rock twice, and still God granted the miracle to help His people. The Lord will always choose to fulfill the greatest cause, which is to touch His people. The sad thing is that the Lord wanted to bring Moses into a new realm of being like Him. Adam lost the power of creating with his speech. This potential would not be approached again until the second Adam, Jesus Christ. Now, of course, this ability has been passed unto us, Christ's siblings. He desired to give Moses the ability to move God by speaking. This is something that the Lord has given you and me. We can move obstacles and mountains with the power of our words.

For this reason, neither Moses nor Aaron could lead the children of God into the promised land. If we, as leaders, can't go to the next level, then there is no way that we can lead the people of God to the next level spiritually, financially, or physically. God will raise up someone who is willing to change and grow according to His demand.

Jesus is metaphorically the Rock. We are required to understand that Jesus was only smitten once, which resulted in the water of life flowing freely to mankind. God told Moses to strike the rock in the eyes of the people so that God could be honored in the mind of the people. God has not smitten Jesus twice. We are not supposed to smite Christ again. We are to simply speak to the Rock and from Him will stream the rivers flowing with life. From Christ flows healing rivers, financial rivers, peace rivers, deliverance rivers, salvation rivers, and "whatever you need" rivers.

This is a great proverb and strong warning to all who desire to work with God. Never do what you think is right; do what you know the Lord is leading you to do. If you live by assumption and presumption, you will find yourself facing the same end as Moses and Aaron. They were not allowed to enter into the Promised Land!

CHAPTER 3

SANCTIFICATION

Those who do wickedly against the covenant he shall corrupt with flattery...

Daniel 11:32, KJV

Christian strength is equivalent to Christ-like character. In studying church history, we see numerous ministers of faith and power who, during their prime time of ministry, blazed the earth with the glory of God. But towards the end of their ministries, any flaws in their character came to the surface and often brought great shame to the Body of Christ and the name of Jesus.

All too familiar are the tragic reports of A.A. Allen, with his drinking problem, and William Branham, who in the last days of his ministry got off course and believed that he was Elijah. These men and others found themselves shipwrecked by the weakness of their humanity and lack of character. We shouldn't look down at the mistakes of these wonderful men of God who ministered with all sincerity; instead, we should learn from their experiences. I believe that God allowed these men to pave a road for our generation. In my study, it was apparent that in each of these leaders' lives, who experienced failure, there was a place where Godly character was at a deficit.

THE CHARACTER MUST BALANCE THE GIFT

If a person's character doesn't balance out their gift, it can be very destructive to them and those around them. The Bible speaks of people who have a form of Godliness and deny the power of God. However, in these last days, I have also seen people with the power of God but who lack the soundness of Godliness.

Daniel 11:32 describes people who have the strength to resist the flattery of the spirit of antichrist through their intimate knowledge of God. This is an unmovable and courageous strength; a strength that will not allow you and me to walk past evil without addressing it. Godly strength keeps you and me from doing anything contrary to the character of God. Most of the time we hear preachers teach from this scripture and totally leave out the fact that people must have strong character to handle the exploits of God. We have disregarded the fact that being strong is necessary for carrying a powerful anointing.

When Paul wrote a letter to Timothy, giving him instruction on how to pastor the churches in his territory, he listed in 1 Timothy 3 the requirements of church leadership. In this chapter, we find out that men of God must have their families and character in order. If these standards were truly applied today, sadly, many of our modern-day church leaders would be asked to sit down until the character of Jesus was formed in them. I am not saying that we can't do anything for God until we're completely perfect, but we should be progressively growing into the likeness and image of Jesus.

The gifts and callings of God are exciting, but just because you're anointed and have a gift doesn't release you from the obligation of having godly character and being transformed into the heart, mind, and righteousness of God.

Paul never said to Timothy, "Don't neglect your gift and don't worry about your character." He put more importance on the character of a minister than he did on the gifts of the minister. Many ministers have thrown out the gifts of God because they were disappointed in certain people who never took the time to develop their character in the same manner as they concentrated on the anointing and the gifts. In the days to come, God is not going to allow us to get away with being "flaky, fly-by-night miracle workers." He has placed a higher demand on our generation because of the example that we have had from the pioneers of the faith.

When I was first developing in the use of the gifts of the Spirit, I ran across some very serious personal character flaws in my life. Fortunately, I had a pastor who took the time to help when he saw these possible snags. He would tell me, "Character will take you further than your gifts." His exhortation caused me to pray a prayer that every sincere person who desires to be used of God should consider praying. My prayer was simple, "Father, don't allow me to be exalted or use these gifts until my character can handle it." For three years, the prophetic anointing left, the healing anointing left, and my character started to be formed.

Today, I thank God for those very difficult three years. I could have gone a long way on just the gifts. Yet, my heart would have been about me and not about loving God and loving people. Most likely doors would have opened, but they only stay open through Christ-like character.

I NEVER KNEW YOU

I once heard it said that it is the little things we do in private that are the things that really count. The things that no one will ever know are the things that give success in life. Spending time in prayer, reading the Word of God, and keeping the Word of God in your mouth, all bring public rewards from God. As we spend time with God, we are transformed inwardly. When we read the Word, we see the character of God develop within us. As we keep our tongues from evil, we change the world around us.

> But we all, with unveiled face, beholding as in a mirror the glory of the Lord, are being transformed into the same image from glory to glory, just as by the Spirit of the Lord.
>
> 2 Corinthians 3:18, NKJV

The Word of God is our mirror. As we look into the glory of the Word, we are transformed into the likeness of Jesus. When Moses returned from the mountain where he received the Ten Commandments, having spent forty days with God, his face shown with the glory of God. This same thing happens to us inwardly while we spend time with God. One day, all who have given their lives to Jesus will walk into Heaven and behold the face of Jesus, at which time He must be able to recognize Himself in us.

The Lord once gave me a word saying, "The world thinks that they can clone My creation, but I will cause confusion to come upon them as they try to build their tower of knowledge to achieve God-like status. In the days to come, I will show them what cloning truly is. The fall of man has put me into a place of not simply being a Creator but also being a Redeemer, Regenerator, and the Master Cloner. I will raise up a people who have the same spiritual DNA as my Son. I have created you from My very image and likeness. The devil and all of his sorcerers will not be able to imitate this. What is it for a man to reproduce what has already been made? What is it for him to take the temporal and regenerate the temporary? Only I can take of nothing and cause life to come about. I am able to cause what is temporal to become eternal. I will cause what is natural to become supernatural. I will cause the carnal to become spiritual, for every cell of your being is pulsating with the glory of My image."

> Many will say to Me in that day, "Lord, Lord, have we not prophesied in Your name, cast out demons in Your name, and done many wonders in Your name?" And then I will declare to them, "I never knew you; depart from Me, you who practice lawlessness."
>
> Matthew 7:22-23, NKJV

We can't afford to disregard the importance of being Christ-like for anything of this world—not fame or riches. Take the time, for Christ's sake, to be formed into His image and likeness. In the end, all that matters is that you look like Jesus. Who do you want to be like? Who do you look like?

PRACTICAL APPLICATION

Discipline in seeking the Lord is necessary to develop Christian character. In my personal routine, I cover three important disciplines that help my transformation into Christlikeness continue to develop. I believe that Jesus was a professional of the highest degree. He did everything with the greatest of care. So, I believe Jesus has the right to be called a pro. With this simple understanding in my mind, I thought of an incredibly easy acronym: P.R.O. This stands for pray, read, and obey each and every day of your life.

FASTING

By adding fasting to a PRO routine, your flesh will promptly come under the submission of the spirit-man within. Fasting is the quickest way to get rid of the old man, old habits, and protect the spirit-man. You know that old man, the one who gets angered easily and loses control. He is the one who lusts after the things of the world. If you have been feeling dry and separated from God, most likely you are in desperate need of a fast. If you feel out of control in your flesh, fasting will bring your flesh to attention.

Fasting starves the addictive behaviors and ungodly appetites that would easily cause you to be shipwrecked. When a person begins to fast, they become aware of the awesome power of the Holy Ghost present within to transform them. Fasting brings victory over spiritual lethargy and complacency; it will stir a revival in your heart for the things of God and His Kingdom.

Fasting is much more than just going without food. We must starve the craving of the flesh by not feeding its desires, and, in turn, feed the spirit-man with spiritual food instead. If you go without eating and you don't replace the meals with prayer or reading, it is only a diet. Fasting is not to lose weight. Nor is it a means for you to climb the positional ladder in God's Kingdom, but it causes you to come closer to God in your perspective. Your ability to hear God is sharpened and you will tap into a source of divine power that has always been available to you. Sin-nature and consciousness have kept us from drawing near to and living the fullness of Christ's stature. Many men of God, such as John G. Lake and William Branham, walked in power because of their lifestyle of prayer and fasting. John G. Lake was a man of fasting and prayer. William Branham would fast and pray three days before each crusade. Jesus was empowered after fasting.

> Now when the devil had ended every temptation, he departed from Him until an opportune time. Then Jesus returned in the power of the Spirit to Galilee, and news of Him went out through all the surrounding region.
>
> Luke 4:13-14, NKJV

The Holy Ghost drove Jesus into the wilderness, where He fasted for forty days, being full of the Spirit. After the temptation of the devil was completed for that season, He came out not only full of the Spirit, but empowered! Through fasting, Jesus received the strength to resist the devil and the power to change the world.

> But He said to them, "I have food to eat of which you do not know." Therefore the disciples said to one another, "Has anyone brought Him *anything* to eat?" Jesus said to them, "My food is to do the will of Him who sent Me, and to finish His work."
>
> John 4:32-34, NKJV

Jesus understood the purpose of fasting and sacrificed earthly food for the sake of doing the work of the Father. When we're fasting, God makes His will known and gives us the goods to get the job done.

PRACTICAL INSTRUCTION FOR FASTING

If you have never fasted, I would suggest starting off with missing one or two meals on the same day, substituting it with prayer and reading the Word of God. It is better to eat breakfast and fast your lunch and/or dinner. Next time, gradually increase the number of days. I would caution you not to fast thirty or forty days without a confirmation from God to do so and a guarantee that you are physically healthy and fit.

Before you begin, determine the length of time you will fast. Pray and establish goals for the fast. Ask God for the strength to endure and to complete the fast. When the set time is finished, thank God for the desired results.

Don't make it complicated. Some people expect an angel to stand at the end of their bed and wake them up every morning and give them the fresh word from Heaven to solve their problems. Everything that we do as Christians is by faith. We started in faith; we must continue to live by faith. Don't change it now. We must end in faith.

Many people get frustrated when they don't get their answer during the fast. I usually won't see the breakthrough I'm seeking until after the fast is completed. I learned that unless God leads me to continue the fast; it is best for me to finish it with thanksgiving on my lips, receiving the breakthrough by faith before it manifests. It has worked out well for me every time. Many of you may have a different result, but don't get uptight. Just remember that God is moved by faith and not by works.

CHAPTER 4

AUTHORITY & POWER

But as many as received him, to them gave he power to become the sons of God, even to them that believe on his name.

John 1:12, KJV

God gave power to those who received Him. In this scripture, the word power (*exousia*) means to have authority or delegated influence. God has given you and me His authority. This authority is given to us when we are born again. When you asked Jesus into your heart to be your Savior and Lord, you received the power to represent Jesus here on Earth and the power to be transformed into a child of God. To receive Jesus is not a passive thing; it is intense. It is not just accepting Him into your life; it is a matter of taking hold of Him with all your might and every fiber in your soul.

HOLDING ON

Holding on to Jesus with all of our hearts is what causes lasting change in our lives. Some think that they can try God. There is no such thing as trying God. There is only getting a good grip and holding on to God. When you get a good grip on Jesus, you can't help but be transformed. Metamorphosis is the result. Just as a chameleon holds onto a rock or a branch and takes on the appearance of the object, you and I are transformed into Christ as we hold on.

Don't miss the power in this scripture. Let's read it again.

> But as many as received him, to them gave he power to become the sons of God, even to them that believe on his name.
>
> John 1:12, KJV

So many Christians are under circumstances and problems that they could overcome if they knew who they are. Let this identity become grounded deeply inside of you. Most believers have a hard time relating themselves to Jesus as they read the Bible. It is easier and more widely accepted to see yourselves as Peter, the one who denied Jesus, or doubting Thomas. I say no! There is a supernatural regeneration taking place in us as long as we hold unto Jesus. You are changing daily!

> Not that I have already attained, or am already perfected; but I press on, that I may lay hold of that for which Christ Jesus has also laid hold of me.
>
> Philippians 3:12, NKJV

Paul himself was not already perfect, nor already the mature image of Christ, but he was determined to push for the promise of being like

Christ. Nothing can separate us from the love of God. Our high call is to be like Jesus. He has taken hold of me and I am trying to get as much of a grip on Him as I can, which is the same as Paul's goal.

THE BADGE OF AUTHORITY

Exousia, which means authority, is to a Christian as a badge is to a police officer. Police officers operate under delegated influence. The enemy exercises his power when given the opportunity, but his authority is limited to what we allow. The devil desires to take your badge like he stole Adam's badge in the Garden of Eden, and just as many others have allowed him to do to them. If he has control over your body, your family, or your finances; then it's time to take it all back!

The devil should not be able to freely come to your home to steal, kill, and destroy without some form of conflict from you. He shouldn't be able to come into your life and take whatever he wants. You have authority over him. For example, a police officer can stand in the middle of the street and stop the traffic with just a flash of his badge. Any person who may be walking or driving in the route of the officer will stop because they know that his badge represents authority. You and I must see that God has given us this same level of authority as a Christian. You and I are the ones who have God's delegated authority on earth.

Every believer has the authority to tread upon serpents, scorpions, and the entire kingdom of darkness through the authority of God. This is the same authority that we must use in order to stand morally and to maintain emotional strength. It is the power to live a holy life through the Holy Spirit who lives inside of us. Each believer has a double portion anointing; the first is for personal freedom and the second is for going about and doing good.

But you shall receive power when the Holy Spirit has come upon you; and you shall be witnesses to Me in Jerusalem, and in all Judea and Samaria, and to the end of the earth.

Acts 1:8, NKJV

The Holy Spirit's first point of contact with man in a personal way was when He came to live in us, at which time He released exousia into our lives. For this second encounter in Acts 1:8, the key word is *upon*. The Spirit of God comes *upon* us for work and accomplishment. This is the power to destroy yokes and break burdens. The Greek word is *dunamis* (do"-nam-is), miraculous power or force.

God has given us the power to be His witnesses, a witness of the resurrection of Jesus, and to enforce the good works of God. The key to winning the lost is to show that Jesus is still alive. As long as we accept the commission to be a witness for Jesus' sake, this power will be released to us as believers. There are many who believe that miracles, the power of God to set the captive free and confirm that Jesus rose from the grave are not for today. I would challenge you to look at the harvest of souls, allow yourself to be filled with the compassion of Jesus for the lost, and do whatever is necessary to reach them. Watch out for teaching that tells you that miracles and the power of God are void and unnecessary. The New Testament is very clear that signs and wonders testify of the living God. Anything that hinders the Gospel from going forth in power and fullness, in the way it is intended, is an enemy of the cross. Unbelievers came out to meet Jesus when they heard of His miracle working power. You should expect this same thing to happen when you trust the Holy Spirit to empower you to help the needy.

Then Peter said to them, "Repent, and let every one of you be baptized in the name of Jesus Christ for the remission of sins; and you shall receive the gift of the Holy Spirit. For the promise is to you and to your children, and to all who are afar off, as many as the Lord our God will call.

Acts 2:38-39, NKJV

Everyone has been called, everyone is called to be baptized in the name of Jesus, and every one of us must receive the gift of the Holy Spirit. You and I are called by God to be a witness of His resurrection power, regardless of our denominational or social background. Every Christian is to be a witness of the resurrection of Jesus.

MAGNUM

To give you an understanding of the second portion of the anointing (dunamis), let's go back to our first analogy of the police officer. The one officer represents thousands of other officers and a whole judicial system. If this doesn't stop an offender, and he makes the choice to ignore the officer's authority and instructions, that officer must judge whether deadly force is needed. There are two reasons for deadly force: the officer's life is in danger or the public is in danger. If deadly force is needed, the officer has a gun to respond to the need. For the sake of our analogy, we will call this gun "dunamis." The power of this gun will help him keep the peace.

If the devil challenges our authority and tries to ignore the many other officers on our side, we are compelled to use deadly force. The devil is a dangerous criminal and cannot be ignored or treated with mercy. There is only one response to his criminal activities: they must be destroyed.

AUTHORITY THROUGH THE WORD

The Word of God is a wonderful weapon of spiritual warfare and power. The best example of this is found in Luke 4. It is the story of when Jesus was confronted by the devil regarding His identity as the Son of God. In Luke 3:22, the Holy Spirit descended upon Jesus and the voice of God came from Heaven declaring, "You are My beloved Son; in You I am well pleased." In chapter 4, the Holy Spirit led Jesus into the wilderness.

Just a side note, some of you who feel dry, as if you are in the wilderness, could be experiencing God setting you up for a promotion! Look through the Bible and see what happened to the people who were driven into the wilderness by God. They were promoted shortly afterward. Red dot yourself during these times, checking your emotional and character growth along the way, so that you may emerge out of your wilderness possessing the glory of the Lord.

While Jesus was in the wilderness, He became subject to several temptations. Each of them strategically plotted out to crush His identity as the Son of God. The first was when Jesus had just finished His forty-day fast. The devil tempted Him to turn some nearby stones into bread. Jesus resisted by proclaiming the written Word and overcame the temptation.

SELFISH MOTIVATION TEST

It was not wrong for Jesus to use His miracle working power. But it would have been wrong for Him to use it at the devil's command. It was a test of using the power of God for selfish gains. As you develop in your spiritual gifts, watch out for this temptation. Jesus answered him, saying, "It is written, 'Man shall not live by bread alone, but by every word of God'" (Luke 4:4, NKJV). This was an awesome use of the *logos* Word (reasoned speech). Jesus had the Word written in His heart, so He was able to reply to the devil through reason.

CHALLENGED FOR AUTHORITY

Even after Jesus refused the devil's command, the devil was still not willing to give up. So, he took Jesus to a high mountain and showed Him all the kingdoms of the world in a moment of time. He could not have shown Jesus all the kingdoms from one vantage point. I believe that the devil showed Jesus a form of his power, the glory of dominion that he stole from Adam. The devil had the audacity to say to Jesus, "All this authority I will give You, and their glory; for *this* has been delivered to me, and I give it to whomever I wish. Therefore, if You will worship before me, all will be Yours" (Luke 4:6-7, NKJV). Jesus, knowing that the devil had no authority over Him answered and said to him; "Get behind Me, Satan! For it is written, You shall worship the Lord your God, and Him only you shall serve" (Luke 4:8, NKJV). Again, Jesus had returned a bruising blow to the devil with the logos (the reasoned speech).

This is the test that Adam failed. It might be obvious to us that if we worship the devil, we will lose our authority, but when we give in to sin, we are doing that very thing: giving up our authority.

THE VAIN GLORY TEST

In Genesis, it says that the snake was the most cunning creature in the garden. Well, he is still cunning. Thank God that we are not ignorant of his devices. He came back to Jesus with his last and hardest blow. He brought Jesus to Jerusalem, set Him on the pinnacle of the temple, and said to Him, "If You are the Son of God (again challenging his identity), throw Yourself down from here. For it is written: 'He shall give His angels charge over you, to keep you,' and, 'In their hands they shall bear you up, lest you dash your foot against a stone'" (Luke 4:9-11). This one could have thrown Jesus for a loop. Just think about this temptation: It was Jesus' greatest desire to glorify the Father. What better way than to get the city of Jerusalem's attention through a glorious act? Maybe it was the day that everyone went to the market and if he had plunged Himself down, the whole city would have seen the angels save Him from certain death.

The devil is completely perverted. He took the Word of God and tried to manipulate it to his own advantage. The devil will try to tempt you by getting you to flaunt your gifts and so cause vainglory to come to you. You might hope that man would recognize you as a man or woman of God. Don't fall for this trap! I believe Jesus nearly cut off the devil's head with this next answer, it was such a severe blow that the enemy had to leave. Jesus answering the devil said to him, "It has been said, 'You shall not tempt the Lord your God'" (Luke 4:12).

ENOUGH IS ENOUGH

Each time the devil came to attack Jesus, the Lord used the logos—the written, reasoned word—to combat the enemy. The final time, the enemy decided to use the written Word. Jesus came back at him with what is called a *rhema* (an uttered word). "It has been said" is what Jesus said, rather than saying "it is written." This implies that Jesus heard something said. The Father in Heaven must have seen the perverted devil trying to trick the Son of Man by using the Word of God against Him. I believe the Father sat up in His throne, stretched forth His finger, and said: "Enough is enough. You shall not tempt the Lord your God." Jesus, in His time of need, needed something to help Him through this temptation and God the Father came through. Jesus fought and fought with the logos until He heard the voice of God, which brought the rhema. When He heard the rhema word, it caused faith to rise up within Him.

> So then faith *comes* by hearing, and hearing by the word of God.
>
> Romans 10:17, NKJV

After faith rose in Christ's heart, the devil couldn't stick around. The devil can't stand faith; that's why he hopes that Christians won't hear the voice of God. Jesus received such victory in the wilderness through the logos and rhema word that He walked out of the wilderness empowered by the Holy Ghost. He went in led by the Spirit and full of the Spirit, but when He came out, He came out full of power. Come on, Christians! The Word is near you, even in your mouth, but the power only comes when you speak it. Speak the Word!

AUTHORITY FROM THE ANOINTING

God wants to anoint us with the Holy Ghost and with power just as He anointed Jesus. To be anointed means to have something smeared or rubbed all over. The anointing on us is God, and His power smeared all over us enables us to accomplish what we couldn't do. The anointing is God's super on our natural. Now, I just want to clear up some of the misconceptions people sometimes have concerning the anointing or anointed individuals. Many people believe that the anointing will take care of any weakness in their souls and even cause their character to change instantly. This is a false assumption: soul and character changes only come through the renewing of the mind. Whether it's through trials or study of the Word of God., exchanging your old thoughts for God's thoughts.

ANOINTING OR A GOOD SHOW?

We must have discerning of spirits so that we can know the difference between the anointing and a good show. The anointing brings results. It's not enough to appear to be anointed, we must be anointed. The anointing is for the purpose of doing work in the Kingdom of God. Do yourself a favor; don't ask for the anointing if you're not planning to do extraordinary things with the power that comes with being anointed.

The anointing is an amplifier for the gifts of God. It is life to dead bodies and dead spirits. The anointing is the power that breaks the yokes of bondage. When a person is approved of God, the Holy Spirit will be smeared all over them to lead, teach, and empower them in reaching people or achieving success in any area pertaining to the anointing.

> How God anointed Jesus of Nazareth with the Holy Spirit and with power, who went about doing good and healing all who were oppressed by the devil, for God was with Him.
>
> Acts 10:38, NKJV

The anointing is a result of the Holy Spirit resting upon someone. The Holy Spirit is God, and the anointing is the favor of God. When the Holy Spirit smears you, He walks with you, leads you, and talks to you. When you're anointed with power, the Holy Spirit destroys yokes for you and through you.

Smith Wigglesworth was so anointed that sometimes the people around him would begin to cry out for help because the conviction of the Holy Spirit would come so strongly upon them that they felt like they were going to die. People still get healed while watching the recordings of Kathryn Kuhlman because God anointed her with the Holy Ghost and power. She may have passed on to glory, but the Holy Ghost is still working in the earth. Elisha's bones were so anointed that when some men threw a dead man on them, the man came back to life. Charles Finney was so anointed that, one day, he went to a sewing factory to look around and a revival broke out in the factory.

Miracles will follow the person with the anointing. Jesus went about doing good and healing all who were under the dominion of the devil. The anointing is proof that God is with you and in you.

> It shall come to pass in that day *that* his burden will be taken away from your shoulder, and his yoke from your neck, and the yoke will be destroyed because of the anointing oil.
>
> Isaiah 10:27, NKJV

The anointing is a vital part of the ministry of a Christian. Where the Spirit of the Lord is, there is freedom. Where the Holy Spirit is, there is the burden removing, yoke-of-the-devil-busting power of God. If you want the glory of God, make sure that God is with you. If God is with you, then His anointing will be on you also.

SPIRIT BEING VERSUS BEING SPIRITUAL

> Now concerning spiritual *gifts*, brethren, I do not want you to be ignorant: You know that you were Gentiles, carried away to these dumb idols, however you were led.
>
> 1 Corinthians 12:1-2, NKJV

Most people who operate in the spirit are recognized as being spiritual people... rather than being recognized as people who live in and function from a place in the spirit. There is a difference between being gifted and being a gift. As English readers of the scriptures we have to surrender our understanding to the interpretation or translation of ancient foreign manuscripts. This has been a blessing to us because of our inability to read Greek, Aramaic, or Hebrew. Yet, some things can get lost in translation, such as the mindset behind the words.

For example in 1 Corinthian 12:1, the word gifts is italicized based upon the translators understanding that the Holy Spirit gives gifts. Yet, the primary translation of the word for gifts later in the same chapter is *charisma, which is most often translated as* favor which one receives without any merit of his own or the economy of divine grace. It's the word for GRACE. If you function in the grace of God, it's different than being gifted. Grace is when I receive God's ability for a certain function. What would it look like if you functioned in God's level of favor for healing or God's favor for miracles or God's favor to prophesy?

You are not merely gifted, you are one with Christ. The gift that you received was that you are one with the Lord. This gives you the same grace and favor in which Jesus functioned. To me, this simplifies how to use my faith to cooperate with God. I can fully thrust my faith in functioning in whatever circumstance expecting the same results Jesus would have rather than me having faith that I have the gift that can produce the same results as Jesus. It seemingly takes me out of the equation.

That same verse says, "now concerning spiritual *gifts...*". The word spiritual is the word *pneumatikos,* which means "one who is filled with and governed by the Spirit of God." This portion of the verse is clearly talking about who we are more than what we do. Paul is encouraging us not to be ignorant about the fact that we are spiritual beings not simply spiritually gifted people. The word ignorant according to the Strong's concordance dictionary is agnoéō, ag-no-eh'-o, which means "not to know through lack of information or intelligence; to ignore; to be ignorant. I don't know why I never recognized that ignorance is a byproduct of ignoring. Let's all make a decision together today that we are not going to ignore our spiritual position and condition as Spirit-filled and Spirit-governed believers who function as if Jesus was functioning Himself. You have that kind of grace and favor. It not just what you possess but it's who you are.

You are more than gifted, you are more than anointed. Jesus wasn't just gifted. Jesus was more than simply anointed. Jesus was the gift to the world. Jesus was the anointed one. This is far more than being gifted, you are a spiritual being just like Jesus. You were made in the image of God and redeemed and restored to the favor and grace as the second Adam.

CHAPTER 5

THE GIFTS OF REVELATION

Therefore I make known to you that no one speaking by the Spirit of God calls Jesus accursed, and no one can say that Jesus is Lord except by the Holy Spirit. There are diversities of gifts, but the same Spirit. There are differences of ministries, but the same Lord. And there are diversities of activities, but it is the same God who works all in all. But the manifestation of the Spirit is given to each one for the profit of *all*.

1 Corinthians 12:3-7, NKJV

The first thing that I would like to bring to your attention is that no one speaking by the inspiration of the Holy Spirit could curse Jesus with his or her lips. In the same manner, no one can proclaim that Jesus is Lord without the influence of the Holy Spirit. I want you to pause for a second and say, "Jesus is Lord." Say it again; now say it one more time. Let me ask you a question. Was it hard for you to say that Jesus is Lord? Did your head spin around as if you had lost all control of your faculties? Did you feel the brush of angel's wings and hear the choir of Heaven singing in the background? No? Then why do we expect that to happen when it is time to operate in the gifts of the Spirit? Why do we expect some great manifestation when it is time to reach the one with the power and presence of God? It seems to me that it is God who is doing all of the work anyhow. In actuality, it is very easy to say Jesus is Lord, and yet we are unable to do this without the help of the Holy Spirit. In the same manner, it is easy for us to heal the sick, to cast out devils, or to prophesy. It is the Holy Spirit who enables us to do all of these things. It is just as simple to see cancer healed as it was for you to say Jesus is Lord. As easy as it was for you to say Jesus is Lord, it is just that simple to operate in the gifts of the Spirit. The simplicity is that it's the Holy Spirit who does both: helps you and me say that Jesus is Lord, and helps us see the miracle of healing in a cancerous body.

Paul says in 1 Corinthians 12:4, "There are diversities of gifts, but the same Spirit." The Holy Spirit delivers all the gifts of God to us. The Holy Spirit delivers the word of knowledge, word of wisdom, and all the other gifts of the Spirit. For this reason, we should rely completely on His leading and instruction for the use of the gifts of the Spirit.

INSPIRED REVELATION VERSUS MENTAL REASONING

The gifts of revelation can be difficult to recognize because, when they are received, they must work past the "filter" of our human reasoning. Although they work within the realm of mental reason, they do not need to be submitted to mental reason. Often, impressions or flashes of insight are interpreted as being the imagination. We must train our minds to differentiate between what thoughts are ours and what thoughts are the mind of Christ. The difficult thing is to separate the inspired revelation from mental reasoning. The line is so fine, we could easily say that revelation initiated by God could be vain imagination and vice-versa. The key to deciphering the difference is discernment and understanding, which we receive through the Word, prayer, and the anointing.

In the book, *God's Generals*, a collection of historical facts about men and women of God written by Roberts Liardon, we find insight into William Branham's early years and how his spiritual gift progressed. When William Branham first started operating in the gift of revelation, he didn't immediately understand every vision that he saw. Sometimes he would have to leave the room where he was praying for someone in order to seek the Lord for understanding. He would then return and release the Word and ministry. After some time of going through this type of development, his confidence in the gift increased to the point that he could meet someone for the first time and the Lord would give revelation so distinct that it would shock those receiving the ministry. He frequently called out names, addresses, and illnesses.

It is very important not to become discouraged during times of development of your gifts of revelation. I believe that we can all step into this realm of power and revelation if we are willing to become trustworthy to obey the Holy Spirit. Making mistakes and missing the mark are all part of developing the gifts of revelation. One thing is for sure; you can't miss it if you never step out in faith; nor can you be fruitful in the Kingdom of God if you never take the first step. All of the gifts are developed through the reason of use. The more you use them, the more God trusts you.

GIVE FREELY

The spiritual law of "Give, and it shall be given to you" truly applies here. Why would the Lord entrust someone with the ability to receive names and addresses if that person wouldn't be faithful with revelation of lesser distinction? As you freely give the gift of God, God will find you faithful with little and will give you more. Healing, love, grace, and power are all to be given freely. What good is a gift if it is not used?

> Heal the sick, cleanse the lepers, raise the dead, cast out demons. Freely you have received, freely give.
> Matthew 10:8, NKJV

Trust the Holy Spirit to teach and train you. If He can train you, He can also trust you. The whole relationship between you and God is a relationship of giving through intimacy. Give intimacy to God and He will return to you the same. This is universally the same with money, power, grace, and mercy. Give, and it shall be given to you.

YOUR SPIRIT MAN

As children of God, our intuition or instantaneous comprehension works within the realms of the spirit, connected with our spirit man. The world calls it the subconscious mind because their spirits are dead to God. Their souls are in complete control of their lives. The Christian believer's soul should be submitted to the spirit man and the demand of the Holy Spirit. Our soul, which is that instrument through which our intuition manifests in the natural realm, is submitted to our spirit man, who is joined to the Holy Spirit. Since we are joined to the Spirit of God, and we have the mind of Christ, most of the impressions and images we receive shouldn't be mentally inspired but God-inspired. We are then able to walk as supernatural people.

THE GODHEAD

For too long, we have underestimated what God has entrusted us with. 1 Corinthians 12:5 differentiates the duties of the Godhead. Paul says that there are diversities of gifts, but the same Spirit, and diversities of administration, but the same Lord. Who is our Lord? Of course, it is Jesus.

Then Paul continues by saying there are diversities of operations, but the same God. Let's call God the operator. Then Paul says the manifestation is given to each child of God, but the manifestation comes by the Spirit of God. Here we have every single person of the Godhead represented. The Father, who is in charge of operations, is the one that is saying, "I desire light." The Father is the operator; the chief who initiates the plan. Now, Jesus is the next in line, and He, being the administrator, draws up the blueprints and says light should be bright, it should give heat and illumination in the night. So, Jesus organizes and gives a job description to the command of how everything should look and function. The Father says, "I want light," and Jesus describes what light looks like. Jesus does not manifest the light nor does the Father manifest the light. Who brings the manifested light? The Holy Spirit! So, we see every single person of the Godhead is involved in creating light.

GREATER WORKS

This is where you and I come into play; how we become involved in the work of the Godhead. John 14:12 says, "He who believes in Me, the works that I do he will do also; and greater *works* than these he will do also, because I go to My Father." Jesus was preparing to go on to the Father and delegate His work unto us. The only qualification He places on His succession plan is to believe in Him. Through our belief in Him, we shall do the same and greater works than Him, all because He left to go to the Father.

In verse 13, He says, "Whatever you ask in My name, that I will do."

Now, our God is not a man that He should lie. If He says that He will do something, we must believe that a mountain would cast itself into the sea before God's word would not come to pass. Verse 17 goes on to say that "He (the Holy Spirit) dwells with you and will be in you." This is good news, because from the time that the Holy Spirit comes to live within us, we no longer live just by our ability but through the power of the one who resides within us.

John 14:19 says, "The world will see Me no more, but you will see Me." If the world will no longer see Jesus, how does God expect the world to be attracted or drawn unto Him? God will reveal himself to us, within us, and through us to a hurting and dying world. We will be transformed into His image; an image of God that can be seen.

In verse 20, we see the Father as the operator, Jesus as the administrator, and the Holy Spirit as the one who manifests what the operator declares. As we read on, we get an understanding of our position, as a whole, in Kingdom authority. We understand why God says that whatever we ask on earth will be done in Heaven by the Father. Jesus says that He is in the Father. As you look at the diagram on the following page, you will get a clear picture of this scripture. We have the Father, then Jesus the Son, and then He states that we are in Him. As you see from the diagram, we have the Father, the Son, and then you. As we read the passage further, Jesus says, "I am in you." In other words, the Comforter is in you. Yes, the Holy Spirit is in you. Jesus said (paraphrase), "I am no longer. I am removed unto my Father. I am at the right hand of the Father interceding for you." Who takes His place? That's right, you and I do! Jesus also said (paraphrase), "I am in the Father, you are in Me, and the Holy Spirit is in you." Now that Jesus is no longer in the earth and removed from His earthly duties, we must take His place of administration. Jesus has delegated His administrative authority to us here on earth as He is in Heaven.

FATHER

SON

YOU

HOLY
SPIRIT

OBEDIENCE

For this reason, we must obey His voice and His leading. We cannot do it on our own. We must listen to what God is saying. God doesn't ask us to throw away our own personalities. Jesus had His own personality in what He did. God is not asking us all to be robots or to be inhuman. All He wants is for us to do His work with His heart and His intentions. He is the One who says, "Tracey, go and lay hands on that lady or call that man over here." Then, when they come, I have to listen for further instruction. If He does not give me detailed instruction, I can step out according to my faith. He might say, "I want you to lay hands on him or her." Sometimes He says, "I do not want you to lay hands on them." Sometimes, He says, "You are to stomp your foot and they shall be healed," or, "Blow on him or her and they will be touched."

Many times, I didn't do what the Lord had asked of me. I remember there was a time that I was at a meeting, and the minister called on a few people to help him pray for a demon-possessed man. For a while, I just stood back and watched, then the Lord spoke to me saying, "Hit him in the stomach." Some may have jumped at this opportunity, but I was a little intimidated by this command and refused to obey. I remembered Smith Wigglesworth, who hit people with glorious results of healing and deliverance, but I just couldn't work past the fear in my mind. I was bold, but this was just too wild for me at the time. So, I compromised. I walked up to the man, balled up my fist and stuck it into his stomach. I pushed with very little force and said, "Be free." The man received some freedom by the time everyone was done praying for him, but he was not completely free. Since then, the Lord has never asked me to do that again, but if He does, I will obey. So, if you're in our meeting and I hit you, just know that it's the Lord! I don't think that God does that all of the time, but I do think that there are times that God asks us to do things contrary to our understanding. I would say that hitting, or any other dramatic gesture, is the exception to the rule.

A MIND TO HELP PEOPLE

God wants His people to do the work. Don't be afraid to step out in faith, even if you don't understand everything that God is prompting you to do. He is a loving and merciful God. Whatever it takes to touch people is what He is interested in. Let us not lose His heart by getting caught up in the gifts or caught up in how uncomfortable it can be. It is all about building the Kingdom and reaching the lost. Let us not lose God's heart in our zeal to be used of God. I am sure it was uncomfortable for Jesus when He spat on the ground, mixed it with dirt, and put it in a blind man's eyes as He focused on God's will. The blind man that Jesus healed didn't care that Jesus spat in dirt and made mud when his eyesight was restored. Everyone that witnessed this miracle may have said, "Oh, He spat," but the person being healed probably thought, "I don't care, spit on me, and pinch me, anything... as long as I get healed and set free." People get caught up on the methods more than the results. "Straining at gnats," is how the Bible refers to it. This is what the Pharisees did. This is what unbelievers do; they do not see the end result. But God has called us to great things, things that our natural minds will not always understand.

OVERCOMING FEAR OF FAILURE

As long as you are joined to the Father, the Son, and the Holy Spirit, you can step out in faith and not bring harm to anyone. That is, as long as your heart is sincere. Do not be afraid to step out and miss it. The fear of failure is the biggest thing that hinders people from reaching the lost. If you can get past the fear of failure, God can take you to unlimited places. You and I are afraid to be shamed, look bad, or have people exclaim that you missed it. It is not an easy thing to step out. You must fight the fear of failure. At times, we are our worst enemy. For this reason, it is important to know who we are in accordance with; God's opinion, not man's opinion. You are wrapped up in God and filled with His very presence. He loves you so much that He surrounds you and dwells in you. He loves you so much that He gave you authority, and then He gave you power to back the authority given you. So now that you know you have a badge and a gun, you are ready to pull the hammer back and take care of business, so to speak.

SPIRITUAL GIFTS, NOT OFFICES

In 1 Corinthians 12:8, Paul describes the different gifts to which we have access. Every child of God is called to operate in spiritual gifts, to proclaim the good news as a witness of Christ's resurrection. This is not a matter of an official calling to minister to the church in a leadership capacity, but these gifts are necessary to function as effective witnesses of Christ. The only requirements are to be born again, filled with the Holy Spirit, and have a faith that God wants to move people through your life. God has delivered to every believer this level of faith. Jude calls it our common salvation level of faith. Please don't confuse these spiritual gifts with the motivational gifts listed in Romans 12, nor with the spiritual offices that are listed in Ephesians 4:11. For example: a person called to the office of a prophet will operate in the gift of prophecy, but people that operate in the gift of prophecy aren't necessarily called to the office of a prophet. It is not necessary to be called to one of the five offices of church government to be used of God. As a believer, you have a ministry.

> And these signs will follow those who believe: In My name they will cast out demons; they will speak with new tongues; they will take up serpents; and if they drink anything deadly, it will by no means hurt them; they will lay hands on the sick, and they will recover.
>
> Mark 16:17-18, NKJV

The ministry of the believer has been a neglected ministry, and I believe that the body of Christ has suffered from the lack of teaching and activation of the believer. The believer has access to the Holy Spirit and His gifts just as the church's governing offices. I truly am convinced that if believers will begin to step into their function under the ministry of the believer, that the church as a whole would be able to affect more people in a shorter amount of time than if God has to wait for one of the five-fold ministry gifts to touch everyone who needs ministry. The problem has been that we have relied too much on the five-fold ministry for actual ministry, instead of demanding that the five-fold train up the saints for the work of the ministry.

> For the equipping of the saints for the work of ministry, for the edifying of the body of Christ, till we all come to the unity of the faith and of the knowledge of the Son of God, to a perfect man, to the measure of the stature of the fullness of Christ.
>
> Ephesians 4:12-13, NKJV

It is easy to miss the whole point of the five-fold ministry if the ministry focus is not to train disciples. The only way the church is going to have victory in the final hour is for the body of Christ to train believers into disciples. Only through activating attendees into believers and believers into disciples will the church step into perfection.

WHEN IS THE GIFT GIVEN?

Every Christian has been given specific spiritual gifts for reaching and ministering. Throughout the course of my walk with God, I have experienced the blessing of being used in most of the gifts of the Spirit. You will not always operate in all of them on a regular basis, but there are certain gifts that God has entrusted to each person. I believe that the gifts of the Spirit are delivered through connecting with the Holy Spirit at salvation, at the time of being filled with the Holy Ghost, by the laying on of hands, or when an individual has a special encounter with the Holy Ghost.

For instance, William Branham didn't receive his gifts of revelation and healing until after he had been ministering for some years, when the angel of the Lord appeared to him in the forest. Kathryn Kuhlman didn't see anyone healed in the first years of her ministry. Healings began to take place after a revelation of her dependency on the Holy Spirit. The Lord may have already imparted the gifts to you that enable you to effectively reach the lost, but often there is a time of revelation that needs to happen for you which will bring the gift or gifts to the surface.

COVET EARNESTLY

God has placed a wonderful emotion in your soul called passion, or, as the Bible calls it, zeal. 1 Corinthians 14:1 uses the word *zeloo* (dza'-lo'-o), which means to have warmth of feeling for or against, or to covet earnestly. The Ten Commandments tell us not to covet anything that belongs to someone else, but here God speaks of another law, which gives us the freedom to covet the things of the Kingdom of God. God can speak to you through pure desires, meaning, if you have a desire to be used, it is most likely God's idea rather than yours. As long as you are seeking to know God and His Kingdom, your motives will be pure. If your motives are not right, you may find yourself very frustrated. If you are seeking God and delighting in Him, you will be able to help many people! God just might shock you with what He will do with you and through you.

> Delight yourself also in the LORD, and He shall give you
> the desires of your heart.
>
> Psalms 37:4, NKJV

When you delight yourself in the Lord, the Lord will bless you with the things that you desire. It is easy to get tripped up by thinking that everything you desire comes from carnal craving. You must realize that now you are a child of God, the Lord creates in you the desire to want the things that He has chosen for you. Philippians 2:13 (NIV) says, "For it is God who works in you both to will and to do for *His* good pleasure." Paul says to covet earnestly, because God has put desires inside of you that benefit the Kingdom of God.

PREPARE FOR ALL OF THE GIFTS

Try not to be distressed when God leads you to do things that you may be unfamiliar with, such as prophecy or praying for a stranger. Just about everything feels uncomfortable when you first try it. Simply remember that, more times than not, God chooses us based upon our availability not our abilities. You may not normally function in the gifts of healings, but God may call on you to operate in that gift from time to time. The will of God is to do whatever is necessary to present Jesus to the earth.

Jesus Himself was, and is, moved by compassion. John G. Lake said that compassion is the key to healing. Ask God to fill your heart with compassion for the lost and broken and watch what happens next. Signs always follow preaching of good news.

Imagine that you are walking down the street, and as you pass a young man, you hear the voice of God or see a quick vision flash before your eyes, showing you that the young man is distressed and is contemplating suicide. At that time, you can continue to go on with your life or choose compassion and take the time to see if there is an opportunity to help him. Don't worry! I will teach you what to do if that happens to you.

LED BY WISDOM

Wisdom is especially needed when operating in the gifts of the Spirit in the secular world. The goal is not to let everyone know that you are gifted. The object is to help people. So, use wisdom as you approach people. I always try to strike up a conversation before I hit them with the Word of the Lord. At that time, I ask the Holy Spirit to open the door. If time is short, I will just walk up to them with a big smile on my face and greet them. People are often very suspicious and nervous, so don't ruin your witness with arrogance. I always ask their permission to tell them the word or what I feel. I use words like, "May I tell you something?" or "May I encourage you with something?" If they are not willing to hear, don't force the door open. Allow the Holy Spirit to open the door, at which point your ministry focus for this person will become intercession. It is important that the Spirit leads us.

LED BY THE SPIRIT

Each one of the gifts has a particular tangible presence of the Holy Spirit that accompanies it. For example, imagine you are standing in line for a concert and the presence of God comes on you as you are waiting to go in. Unless there is a gift of revelation accompanying this presence, you will have to ask the people around you whether or not they are in need. As you become aware of this anointing, it may start to move into your hands. Your hands might turn red and get hot. They may tingle a little. This type of manifestation usually accompanies one of the gifts of power, mainly the gifts of healings. Look around to see if anyone is noticeably ill. If you don't notice anything, then turn to the person next to you and introduce yourself to them, tell them what you are feeling, and ask them if they are in need of prayer. Don't be shy about it. You never know what will happen. Cancer may be destroying someone's body and they will be healed when you pray for them. Do yourself a favor, don't make working with the Holy Ghost so mystical that you become afraid to step out. Avoid being weird or strange. Remove anything that could be a distraction from the message. With that said, there are times when the Holy Spirit's power is extravagant. I am not talking about those moments. I am talking about learned Christian behavior that may be more cultural than God's power manifesting.

Remember, it only takes faith. Right now, where you are, say out loud, "Jesus is Lord." Very easy, wouldn't you say? Remember what 1 Corinthians 12:3 says, "No one can say that Jesus is Lord except by the Holy Spirit." Saying Jesus is Lord is not so mystical, is it? Neither is operating in the Spirit. It is supernatural, but not mystical. Do not forget that just as simple as it is to say, "Jesus is Lord," it is the same to see the sick healed, to receive a word of knowledge or a prophetic word. These, too, can only be done through the help of the Holy Spirit.

READY IN SEASON AND OUT OF SEASON

We should have an understanding of all of the gifts of the Spirit in order to be ready in season and out of season. The Holy Spirit should be able to use us at any time, no matter what is needed, when it is needed, and where you are needed. Some people are intimidated to minister the grace of the Holy Spirit only as far as what is familiar to them. Yet, my hope is that you will become more available to the Holy Spirit's leadings than you are familiar with all the gifts of the spirit. Why? Because growth happens when you are being stretched. Let's say that you are experienced in how the gift of prophecy works, yet you feel a leading to pray for someone who is sick while walking through the supermarket. Right in front of you, a man falls to the floor, clutching his chest. It appears that the man is suffering from a heart attack. Instantly, the Holy Spirit speaks to you, "Go and lay hands on that man and I will raise him up." You step out in faith and he gets instantly healed! The gift of God saved someone's life through the power of God.

If there is no one with the gift of healings in the grocery store, and somebody falls over from a stroke, then God is going to call upon you, not the cashier who does not know Him. You may say, "Healing is not my gift, God!" Well, that day, you may be called on to operate in healing. At any given time, God can call upon you to operate in any of the gifts.

You must have an understanding of them all in order to be prepared for these opportunities. The scripture says that we should not be ignorant of the grace and gifts of the Holy Spirit. The meaning of "ignorant" is not only lacking information, but it includes ignoring information that you should pay attention to.

Some people prophesy once and never prophesy again. When Moses passed by with the prophets, the Spirit of the Lord was released on the people and they prophesied once and never did again. Some of us may operate in a different gift and never operate in it again, but God has delivered unto you at least one of these gifts to operate in on a regular basis. We should never forget that the evidence of the ministry of a believer is to lay hands on the sick and they recover.

We are the CHURCH; the only answer to the problems in the world. We are the body of Christ. I cannot be the eye if I am the toe. I have to be exactly what God has called me to be. When we all work together in the body, then the work of God will be accomplished in us and in the earth. The days are changing, and you can't always wait for one of the five-fold ministers to do all of the work. It is time for the grassroots-believer to be empowered to win souls and change lives.

THE PURPOSE FOR REVELATION

The purpose of the gifts of revelation are to deliver the revelation and interest of God to man. It is purposed to release revelation and understanding to man from God, personally, and for the benefit of others. It is allowing God's intentions, desires, and ideas to be known to man.

CHAPTER 6

THE WORD OF WISDOM

**For to one is given by the
Spirit the word of wisdom.**

1 Corinthians 12:8, KJV

The word of wisdom is supernatural revelation or insight into the divine will and purpose of God, showing how to solve any problem that may arise. So many times in our lives, we operate in the word of wisdom and never realize that it is heavenly wisdom. Heavenly wisdom enables the miracle working power of God to work along with the wisdom given. Very often, words of wisdom do not make sense to the natural mind. I am confident that most of you operate in words of wisdom and have never been able to explain where this insight has come from. Possibly you had a good idea but according to all natural circumstances it seemed it would never work, but something inside of you told you to go through with it anyway. When all was said and done, the plan worked out better than you could have imagined.

Unfortunately, we often overlook these instructional impressions for familiar human reasoning and miss the miracle working power of God. I hope that after reading this chapter you will be more conscious, alert, and aware of any possible revelation from God. Then it won't drop to the floor without you at least praying it through. God has so many things to tell us, but traditional mindsets will resist the Holy Spirit revelation.

PERSECUTION COMES WITH THE CALL

We are either afraid of being persecuted or afraid of being wrong. With these images of misfortune on our mind, many of us have chosen the route of mediocrity; allowing the devil to steal one of the greatest joys of being saved, being able to help someone else. Persecution comes with the call of living as a Christian. The only way to avoid persecution is to be completely self-absorbed, worldly, or deny your love and loyalty towards Christ. I encourage you not to be afraid of persecution and miss the blessing that flows back to you after you have sown it into someone's life.

> "Remember the word that I said to you, "'A servant is not greater than his master.' If they persecuted Me, they will also persecute you. If they kept My word, they will keep yours also.'"
>
> John 15:20, NKJV

Some will persecute us, but then there are those who are in need and desperate for something encouraging. The saved and unsaved are ready to hear the Word of the Lord. Let's give them the unadulterated Word of the Lord. When Jesus said that they would hear our words, He didn't mean the words of our opinion, but the words that we speak from His mouth and throne.

SELF-GENERATING MIRACLE POWER

The purpose of the word of wisdom is to bring heavenly wisdom into earthly circumstances, to bring instruction where it is needed. As soon as the recipient of the word follows the instruction, it instantly brings about power.

For example, I once had hiccups for 48 hours. I tried everything to get them to stop. I tried to scare them out of me. I tried to eat sugar upside down. I even tried breathing into a paper bag. Yes, even holding my breath! Frustrated, I went to bed and woke up with them. The next day as I was driving to church with my wife Nathalie, I said, "Lord, I have to get rid of these hiccups." Then a word of wisdom came to me instructing me to hold my breath for 40 seconds. I thought to myself, I have already tried that! I had tried holding my breath several times before, but not at the order of the Lord. We must follow the Word completely. Encourage the people to whom you minister in the same way. When I held my breath and let go, the hiccups were gone!

I tried so many times in my own wisdom to rid myself of those annoying hiccups, but nothing happened. This time, the Word of the Lord came to instruct me on how I could be set free. Obedience to the word of wisdom released miracle-working power.

WORDS FOR A SOLUTION

If God has instructed you with the word of wisdom and you still have not obeyed what He has commanded you to do, you shouldn't wonder why you haven't received the breakthrough for which you've been praying.

Listen to your Creator, He knows best! Follow His instruction and you will receive God's breakthrough power.

Words of wisdom will not reveal the problem or need to you, but it will reveal the solution. First you will receive the revelation of the problem through natural circumstances, through the word of knowledge, through conversations, or by any natural knowledge. Once you know about a problem, the gift of wisdom can be activated to help with a solution. The recipient of the word will need to act on the instruction to move Heavenly wisdom into motion and heaven will begin to work diligently to bring about the miracle.

The success of the word of wisdom is strictly based upon obedience to that word. The word of wisdom must be obeyed by the receiver for the miracle working power to operate. When you act upon the wisdom that God has given you, God will work a supernatural manifestation for you and change the circumstances.

POWER FOR PROMOTION

Every Christian believer should be able to minister to the lost and hurting through the power of the Holy Spirit. A good friend of mine is a police officer. One day while having lunch with him he explained to me that he sometimes would get very strong feelings or impressions while at work. Often, he would know that someone was lying to him or he would have understanding or wisdom beyond his officer training. I'm sure that some of these things were from his education, but as he described a few instances that occurred I realized that he was not only operating by instinct and instruction, but also in divine revelation. By the end of our conversation, he realized that God wanted to give him revelation while at work as a normal routine. Think about how many lives can be saved if he just happens to be in the right place at the right time. God can warn him of dangerous situations or help him capture a suspect before the call even comes to him. He would be in the right place at the right time through the help of the word of wisdom.

Can you imagine what could happen if you would allow the Lord to be involved in every part of your life through the word of wisdom? If you are an investor, investing will never be the same. If you clean carpets for a living, carpet cleaning will never be the same. One word of wisdom could change your position at work. In a business meeting you could receive the instruction that would change the future of the corporation.

THE KEY TO NATURAL PROBLEMS

"And He said to them, "'Cast the net on the right side of the boat, and you will find some.'" So they cast, and now they were not able to draw it in because of the multitude of fish."

John 21:6, NKJV

This took place after the death and resurrection of Jesus. As far as the disciples were concerned, Jesus had gone away, and they didn't know what to do other than to return back to their work as fishermen. They had been fishing all night and were unable to catch anything. Often words of wisdom apply to natural needs, considering that most of our problems are manifested in the natural realm. Although a person can have spiritual and emotional problems, these still manifest natural effects. So, when you have a word of wisdom from the Lord, it will often deal with the natural difficulties that you are facing in life. Maybe your marriage or relationships, your health, your business, or anything that needs the touch of God.

In Verse 6, we see the word of wisdom, God told them exactly what to do. He gave them the wisdom to bring increase into their lives, a divine revelation of how to solve their problem of lack and bring supernatural increase. At the instruction of the Lord, they cast their nets on the opposite side of where they had been fishing. The increase was so great that they could not bring the reward of their obedience into the boat. Wow! Are you ready for this type of increase in your life? Well, get ready! It shall come if you obey the Lord.

> "Then He got into one of the boats, which was Simon's, and asked him to put out a little from the land. And He sat down and taught the multitudes from the boat. When He had stopped speaking, He said to Simon, "Launch out into the deep and let down your nets for a catch." But Simon answered and said to Him, "Master, we have toiled all night and caught nothing; nevertheless at Your word I will let down the net." And when they had done this, they caught a great number of fish, and their net was breaking. So they signaled to their partners in the other boat to come and help them. And they came and filled both the boats, so that they began to sink. When Simon Peter saw it, he fell down at Jesus' knees, saying, "Depart from me, for I am a sinful man, O Lord!"
> Luke 5:3-8, NKJV

Peter answered the Lord the way so many of us do, "I have already tried it that way." Thank God that Peter didn't stop there. He later replied, "Nevertheless at your word I will let down the nets." This is when the miracle was activated. Peter's obedience to the instruction of Christ activated the Working of Miracles. Words of Wisdom are instructions that unless they are obeyed will not bring about the miracle. This is what makes it different than words of knowledge. Wisdom is the proper application of knowledge. Knowledge is information that has yet to be acted on. Wisdom demands action, while knowledge does not.

I have noticed that, in my life, the word of wisdom comes just at the right time. After trying everything possible to bring about the breakthrough, just when I have exhausted every option, the Lord gives a bit of insight that changes my whole perspective. Many times we react just like Peter did in this scripture, with a feeling of distress and weariness. Nevertheless, we must not forget that when we're in the tunnel the Lord is our guiding light. Just remember that when you're tired of fighting, that's when God runs to the battle.

A REASON TO LIVE

The most exciting thing about this is not that we can receive the word of wisdom for ourselves; the excitement comes when we receive a word for someone else that is in distress. Seeing the hope and joy when you speak a word that brings about the desired change in a life is exhilarating. Look for these opportunities throughout your daily routine. If you see someone distressed, ask the Lord for the opportunity to minister His wisdom to him or her. You will find that in the morning you will be more eager to jump out of bed to prepare yourself in prayer and the Word because you expect to be used during the day, fulfilling the call of God to help someone who is in need.

Don't concern yourself with what to say, the Holy Spirit will give you what to say when the time is right. Often you will find yourself in the middle of a conversation uttering wisdom, a clarity released into your heart at that specific moment. Other times, you will receive insight for a friend or someone during prayer. At these times, it is very important to pray it through before delivering the word to them. You may need to pray for the right time to deliver the word to that person or you may not need to tell them at all. It is very possible that the Lord is showing the solution for the sake of prayer only and you must become their intercessor until the thing that God has shown you comes to pass or until the Lord releases you from the burden. People tend to say things that God didn't tell them to say. Instead of praying what God told them to pray, they talk. Try to stay away from this, because you could offend the person if they are not ready to hear what you have to say. On the other hand, don't be afraid to make a mistake because God will cover your ignorance, but He will not cover your stubbornness until you repent.

THAT'S THE MOTIVE?

Sometimes God gives information, and you may not know what you should do with it. The last thing that you will want to do is to move on it in haste. You should spend plenty of time praying about what to do before you act. I have realized that I often receive information strictly for the purpose of prayer. If you think that the information you have received should be shared, then I encourage you that it is best for the Lord to prepare the heart of the hearer as you are praying for them. Do this while waiting for the right opportunity to share the information with them. If it feels good in your heart and you have peace about it, then you should share it once the opportunity arises. If you make a mistake, pray for more understanding, and look for someone else to bless. Making a mistake is something that must be expected as you develop. You will have less of an opportunity to mess something up if you pray before you speak. If you are motivated by love, God will cover your failures. If someone has negative criticism about what you are attempting to do for the Lord, don't argue with them or justify yourself. Leave it in the hands of the Lord, He will justify you. The only perfect minister so far is Jesus, and we all are pressing toward the pattern of our Savior.

Be confident when you speak on behalf of the Lord and never change your word unless the Lord shows you that you missed it. Most of the time, your first word is right. I will cover more on this in the prophecy chapter. Don't discredit yourself before you're sure that you have missed it. People will always doubt whether your words are true. The worst thing to do is to make sure that you have a way out; this behavior is always motivated by fear. Fear is your enemy and a minister's downfall.

GO TO FLORIDA

For example, I was praying for a friend of mine who was considering a career change. She owned a hair salon, but she desired to move into a new technique in hair cosmetics. She was planning to attend a conference in Florida to learn more about these new techniques. The Lord spoke to me, saying, "Tell her to go to Florida no matter what, and I will bless her." So, I told her. I felt very silly telling her to go to Florida since she had already made up her mind to go.

A few weeks later, she phoned me to ask me to pray about this trip again because all her plans were falling through. She couldn't get a plane ticket, the hotels were booked, and financial problems had arisen. Topping it off, she found out that the same conference was also going to be held in Las Vegas just a few months later. Logic told her to go to the one in Las Vegas to save money and time since she was only a four-hour drive from there. The funny thing about God is that He doesn't operate in the arena of logic. He will tell you to do the most illogical things and have them produce incredible fruit!

DON'T CHANGE YOUR WORD

I agreed to pray again even though I didn't think that the word was off. I was sure that God had given a clear-cut word. I went to a place where I could be alone and clearly hear the voice of God. Just as I stepped into the room and closed the door the Lord said, 'Don't change your word, all of the doors will open up." I immediately went back to the phone and told her what the Lord said. Approximately four hours later she called again and said that everything had opened, even to the point that finances were supernaturally provided for the trip. She went and met great contacts in the business. She has closed her salon and opened a specialty clinic. She is happily in the will of God.

Come on, if you are ever called upon to speak to nations and/or kings in the Name of the Lord you won't have the privilege of second-guessing whether it was from the Lord just because it doesn't line up with human logic or reasoning. How can we judge the angels with our own inferior wisdom? We must have the wisdom of God for ruling and reigning. If you miss it, then be honest. Don't get condemned, just get up, dust off, and move on. People are looking for help, so don't be afraid to help.

HE KNOWS YOUR NEED

"When they had come to Capernaum, those who received the temple tax came to Peter and said, "Does your Teacher not pay the temple tax?" He said, "Yes." And when he had come into the house, Jesus anticipated him, saying, "What do you think, Simon? From whom do the kings of the earth take customs or taxes, from their sons or from strangers?" Peter said to Him, "From strangers." Jesus said to him, "Then the sons are free. "Nevertheless, lest we offend them, go to the sea, cast in a hook, and take the fish that comes up first. And when you have opened its mouth, you will find a piece of money; take that and give it to them for Me and you."

Matthew 17:24-27, NKJV

Even though Peter was caught in a lie, God still worked with him. It is so funny how God will choose the times that you least deserve a blessing to bless you. That way we could never take the credit for such a great breakthrough. Our Lord is the greatest teacher. He will never allow an analogy to go by unused. Peter was lying on behalf of the Lord, claiming that Jesus had paid His tribute when the truth was that the Lord had not paid tribute. Jesus, being a man of integrity, called Peter to the side and gave him a little lesson on integrity. After He exhorted him with words, He also encouraged him in deed.

This was an incredible example of how Jesus chose to submit to the lesser law (of this world) to establish a higher law (of the Spirit). Showing that He had the power to cause every created thing to answer His beckoning call. Why did the Lord choose to have a fish deliver the breakthrough money? I believe it was for Peter's sake. God was working with Peter to give him a new spiritual understanding. The Lord was showing Peter that He was in control and that there was no need to assist God by lying. It was as if the Lord was saying, If I need money, I can even use a fish to bring it to me. Don't try to cover for me, I own all things. God was giving Peter a revelation of His great superiority. Supernaturally, the Holy Ghost caused this fish to have enough money in its mouth to pay the taxes for both Jesus and Peter. The Lord did not say, "Go to the bank and I will supernaturally increase your bank account overnight." He said, "Go fishing." God used what Peter knew about fishing to reveal to Peter His unlimited authority. Peter was a professional fisherman, and I am sure that he understood all that could be known about fishing. God defied the odds and caused Peter to believe. Remember that God gives the word of wisdom for His sake and for those who receive the word. When the breakthrough manifests, faith is increased, and the Lord gets all the glory. That is the reason for our involvement, to give the Lord all the glory.

HOW DO YOU RECOGNIZE THE GIFT?

The word of wisdom is as if God deposits His presence upon and inside of you, which causes clarity to come to your mind. This is the way it comes to me. It may come to you in a different way. Some of you might not be able to relate with my description because it does not feel as super-spiritual or super-spooky as you might think. Clarity comes to your mind, and you know exactly what is going to solve the problem. You know exactly what is going to happen. It is the wisdom from heaven. You may even have tried it before, but it didn't work because the power of the Lord wasn't behind it. It is as if a light bulb just comes on and you realize that you have the solution. God will bring the revelation at the right time. He gives you a divine solution to your problem and you see the problem in a new light, the light of the solution.

CHAPTER 7

THE WORD OF KNOWLEDGE

To another the word of knowledge through the same Spirit.

1 Corinthians 12:8, NKJV

A word of knowledge is supernatural revelation of divine knowledge or insight into God's mind, will, or plan. It is also insight into the plans of others that man could not know of himself. The word of knowledge can bring a breakthrough like nothing else can. It cooperates and functions with other gifts of the Spirit. The word of knowledge rarely operates in and of itself. Sometimes God will give words of knowledge to you as you intercede, yet, outside of prayer, it will activate another gift.

It is never proper to just give a word of knowledge and then leave the person without a solution. I once heard of an evangelist who would call people out of the crowd and only tell the person the symptoms and problems in their body, then have them sit back down. Well, I would rather not have the word of knowledge if all I did was tell someone that they were sick without doing anything about it. Don't forget, in the excitement of receiving a word of knowledge, that it is not the end of ministry to the individual. Look for one of the accompanying gifts of power, revelation, or utterance.

I saw a commercial by a psychic, and this lady was doing nothing other than telling people what was going on in their lives, but she didn't have the words of life in her mouth to truly help them.

THE CROWBAR

The word of knowledge is like a crowbar. It pries open the door of people's hearts to allow the Holy Spirit to move in. This is called the strongman's gospel, named by John G. Lake to describe the gospel preached with power. Jesus used this type of ministry while He was living on the earth.

> Then the woman of Samaria said to Him, "How is it that You, being a Jew, ask a drink from me, a Samaritan woman?" For Jews have no dealings with Samaritans. Jesus answered and said to her, "If you knew the gift of God, and who it is who says to you, 'Give Me a drink,' you would have asked Him, and He would have given you living water."
>
> John 4:9-10, NKJV

Jesus stepped away from religion in this story. He did something that should have never been done by a good Jewish man. The relationship between the Jews and Samaritans was one of disdain. Jews would walk around Samaria to get to the territory on the other side. Jesus did what was uncommon to reach the one. We must follow Jesus' lead in doing what is uncommon. Jesus initially broke many barriers for this one person. He went into Samaria and He talked to a woman in public—not just any woman, but a Samaritan woman.

As we are reaching out to win the lost and change lives, we will have to do as Jesus did. We must be willing to go the extra mile and touch people's lives where they are; no matter what race or social caste system we have to cross. This maneuver by Jesus was so unusual that it caused the Samaritan woman to take note that there was something different about this man, even before the supernatural kicked in.

People should sense that there is something different about us before they see the supernatural side of us. People should know that we are genuine and loving. We must show that we really care. Sometimes, I think that we get so excited about the gifts of the spirit that we forget we are actually dealing with people whose lives are in desperate need. Don't forget that people are not for the practice of your gift, but your gift is for people who have real issues, needs, and hearts.

NEVER THIRST AGAIN

Jesus realized that this woman didn't have the full picture. God is so good to give a gift in order to make sure that we are aware of what He is doing. He draws us by the Holy Spirit. Unfortunately, some people still don't experience enlightenment. The word "gift" is the word *dorea*, which means a gratuity. The Vine's expository says that in the New Testament, dorea is always referred to as a spiritual or supernatural gift.

If the Samaritan woman had understood who was standing in front of her, and the authority that He had, she would have asked for life. If this has happened to Jesus, it will also happen to us. People will not always recognize that you have been sent to them as a change agent. You must be willing to be patient with each person. Jesus showed so much grace with this woman. He could have walked away frustrated with the fact that she didn't understand what was going on, but He chose to be a life giver even though the women didn't ask for help.

A word of knowledge should make you aware of information and details that you previously didn't possess. Many think that a word of knowledge is the gift to study and gain knowledge. I want to make it very clear that a word of knowledge is a supernatural understanding that is given by God to deal with past, present, and even future events.

> But whoever drinks of the water that I shall give him will never thirst. But the water that I shall give him will become in him a fountain of water springing up into everlasting life. The woman said to Him, "Sir, give me this water, that I may not thirst, nor come here to draw." Jesus said to her, "Go, call your husband, and come here." The woman answered and said, "I have no husband." Jesus said to her, "You have well said, 'I have no husband,' for you have had five husbands, and the one whom you now have is not your husband; in that you spoke truly." The woman said to Him, "Sir, I perceive that You are a prophet."
>
> John 4:14-19, NKJV

When this woman heard of the wonderful possibility of never thirsting again, she immediately asked for it. Many times, all people need is a little nudge in the right direction, and the next thing you know, they begin to recognize what is right in front of them. The promise of her never having to come to the well to draw again was so intriguing. When she took the bait, she received the final revelation of who was standing before her with a word of knowledge. The Lord prepared her heart and then pried her heart open just a little further with the word of knowledge. He asked her to call her husband. She replied that she didn't have a husband. Then God opened the floodgate of revelation. "You have had five husbands." I imagine at this point, the woman's face started to turn red and she began to get a little uncomfortable. She realized that she wasn't talking to just an ordinary man, but the Son of Man, a prophet of the Lord. At this revelation, the living water began to flow in her heart, and she was filled with joy and excitement. Overflowing with this living water, she went to her city and caused the people to come out and see the Lord.

THE STRONGMAN'S GOSPEL

The word of knowledge is a wonderful tool for evangelism. Some time ago, I was in the mall and I happened to stop at an Internet kiosk where they were allowing people to surf the net to display their product. I thought that it would be fun to pull up our new ministry website. As I was pulling up our page, the lady working the kiosk came over and started talking to me. While we were talking, I thought to myself, "This would be a great time to open the door to witness to this lady." So, in my heart, I asked the Lord to open the door. Then I pointed out my web page to her and explained that I was a minister. She quickly stated that she was Jewish. Well, of course I asked her if she was orthodox or secular. She stated that her father was Orthodox, but she was not. Instantly, the Holy Spirit spoke to me and said, "She is a lesbian." I was taken a little off guard with the boldness of the Holy Ghost, but sometimes that's the way He is if there is not a lot of time and He wants to take advantage of an opportunity to love someone. I decided to pursue that road. No, I didn't jump out and bash her over the head with every scripture in the Bible against homosexuality. The Holy Spirit won't be able to trust a lot of people with too much revelation because they wouldn't use wisdom when He gives them insight.

WISDOM WINS SOULS

Jesus used wisdom to win souls. Proverbs says that a wise person shall win souls. So, I started asking her questions about her belief system, leading to the subject of homosexuality. After a few minutes of conversation, I finally got her to the point that I could share the Word of God with her. I briefly explained to her about prophetic ministries and that God showed me that she was gay, as well as a few other things in her life. At this point, it was quite fun because she was hanging on every word that I said, and you could see the surprise all over her face. Then the Lord said that He would heal her after I shook her hand. When I told her this, she immediately stuck out her hand to receive her healing. Many people reading this might ask if I made her get down on her knees, repent, and say the sinners' prayer. No, I didn't. However, I did lead her to the Lord. The word of knowledge opened her heart to hear and receive the gospel. This is what John Wimber called power evangelism, and it works.

KNOWLEDGE FOR ACTION

Discernment is crucial when receiving a word of knowledge. There are so many ways to receive a word of knowledge: through dreams, visions, trances, the voice of God, or a knowing (intuition). Remember not to make the gifts too mysterious, they are simple and practical. The things of God are very practical. It's a type of administration of the things of the Spirit. When I say practical, I mean that they are functional for every believer. Knowledge is information that empowers us to accomplish a specific task. When you receive a word of knowledge, it's not just for your information. What you do with that knowledge is administrative.

With knowledge comes an anointing to accomplish. Words of knowledge can be received as the voice of God, by a vision, or by what I call a knowing—where you simply "know that you know," as Benny Hinn would say. It is when you know something as clear as I know that my name is Tracey. The danger of this gift is that you will have the opportunity to mentally process it and, at times, will reason it away. When you receive a word of knowledge, it will sometimes feel like you are instantly filled up with information.

When you tell someone about their life and they don't know you, and they know that you have no way of knowing anything about them except through God, they will easily come to realize that God loves them enough to speak to them through you.

This is such a wonderful way to help people. But please understand that it would be very easy to let a gift like this get out of hand and go to your head. Just remember these three things and you will be all right.

First, you're nothing without Jesus. Secondly, you're not more important than anyone else; God can use a donkey or a rock if He desires. Thirdly, always give God the glory and show public humility through thanksgiving.

In Acts 9:8, we see the works of Ananias, the man who prayed for Saul when he was blind. This is an incredible example of the word of knowledge which came through a vision. Ananias received information that he didn't know before. The Lord showed him the name of the person He wanted him to minister to, as well as the street where the man was to be found. This is a wonderful picture of how and why God moves.

At this point, I am sure that Saul was distressed at losing his sight, which led him to pray to the One who temporarily took his sight. Just a side note, for those people who might read this and think that this is a great example for proving your point that God puts sickness on people. God may have caused him to be blind, but God also caused him to see again. The key to seeing God move on behalf of Saul was that Saul was praying. The people who get the best words spoken over them are usually people who have been talking to God, or people who have others talking to God for them.

After Ananias received the word of knowledge, which got his attention, the Lord began to prophesy to Him. I don't believe that anyone can prophesy without the help of the word of knowledge or some other revelation concerning the past, present, or future. Just receiving the revelation is not prophetic, because the prophecy is a gift of utterance. It is when the word that is to be uttered moves from just revelation to creation. We will cover more of this in later chapters.

SPIRITUAL HUNGER

It's time for us to gain an understanding of the supernatural if we really want to be effective in reaching the lost world. The supernatural is the technology of the future. It will take men and women like Ananias to move the hard-hearted, murdering gang member, or the careless, AIDS riddled prostitute to the altar, or the self-sufficient businessperson to lay everything at the foot of the cross. We must kill the Sunday-as-usual-meetings and turn them into times of refreshing and equipping. Remove the half-digested sermons and feed the people with an eternal purpose. Get out of the suburban fantasy of a nice little church where there will never be any nose-ringed skateboarders or over-grown hippies who reek of smoke or the embezzling success monger. Pastors, if this is your dream and you want an easy ministry without casting out devils and dealing with the undignified, save the world some trouble and turn in your ordination papers, because Christ the Physician is looking for the hurting.

Ananias instantly stepped out to accomplish the word that God had commissioned him to perform. When he stepped into the room that Saul was in, he approached him, laid his hands on him, and prayed for the healing virtue of God to set Saul free. Instantly, the power of God moved on Saul and the darkness fell from his eyes.

STRAIGHT STREET ENCOUNTER

We see three gifts of the Holy Spirit working in conjunction to accomplish the will of God. First, the word of knowledge. The Lord said to Ananias, "Go to Saul at Straight Street." The second was the gift of prophecy. The Lord said, "He is My chosen vessel to go to the Gentiles." Thirdly, was the gift of healing. Ananias prayed for Saul's eyes and the scales fell. In this example, other categories of the gifts are activated through the word of knowledge. First came a gift of revelation; second, a gift of utterance; and third, a gift of power.

Do not just walk up to someone and say, "Your child is in jail," and then walk away. You have to give them something from the treasures of Heaven to hold on to, some hope and life. The word of knowledge does not pry open the door and leave it open for the wind and draft to come in, but it opens the door so that they can be ministered to.

The word of knowledge often feels like a half full glass of water, and then God pours more water in until I am overflowing. I can see things one way, God gives a word of knowledge, and suddenly I realize that God sees it all very differently. Sometimes it comes as a still small voice. For example, in one case, God spoke to me concerning a lady; when she was a little girl, she had experienced a supernatural encounter with Him. That was the word of knowledge. After that, the revelation came.

I saw her standing by her bed and the Lord showed me a great deal of details in the room, and the Lord continued to speak a word of healing and restoration to her.

At times, I will feel the power of God rushing down my leg, then I will say to the person that I am praying for, "Do you have a problem in your right leg?" I share the knowledge that God has released to me through a tangible anointing. At the time, I can feel it physically. This is a natural manifestation of the word of knowledge. Seek the Lord for more understanding regarding the tangible anointing that accompanies the word of knowledge. A tangible anointing will help confirm that God is working.

CHAPTER 8

DISCERNING OF SPIRITS

To another discerning of spirits.

1 Corinthians 12:10, NKJV

Discerning of spirits is the supernatural ability to distinguish between spirits, good or evil. It is also the ability to know the mind of man. Many times, we will go to a new territory to minister, and the Holy Spirit will show us the spiritual darkness and principality that controls that territory. Also, what type of angels He has released to that territory to bring the breakthrough for the Kingdom of God. With regional information, you can understand how to reach the one whom you are sent to reach.

Remember that all of the gifts of revelation work with the reasoning faculties of your mind. But we are never to allow them to become reasoned thought or processed imagination. The only reason they must first come through your mind is that God has made us free moral agents. If God would ever override our decision-making abilities, it would be practically the same as demon possession. Another reason is that we must filter every revelation that we receive through the sifter of the written Word of God. A revelation will never oppose or be contrary to the Bible. It must fit within the puzzle of the sure word of revelation.

Many people are receiving revelation that is contrary to the Word of God and claim to have a discerning spirit. As you speak and receive revelation from the Lord, the logical part of your mind should be going through all of the scriptures to confirm the revelation. If you can't think of a scripture right off hand to confirm what you are discerning, it is best to put it on the shelf until you know that it is Godly. Know that the purpose for this caution is not to be controlling or legalistic, it is so that everything we do and say is done in the character, love, and Name of Jesus.

I SEE YOU

Discerning of spirits is very similar to the word of wisdom and word of knowledge in that it will come through dreams, visions, intuition, impressions, trances, or the voice of God. This gift is very easy to become carried away with. After seeing one demon, people tend to become demon conscious. I believe that God is showing the strategic placement of angels more than demons. On the same note, it is important to know Satan's plans in order to defy the plots of the devil.

> Lest Satan should take advantage of us; for we are not ignorant of his devices.
>
> 2 Corinthians 2:11, NKJV

The Lord is interested in helping us keep the upper hand on the kingdom of darkness. So, He gave us this special gift to thwart his plans. Many church splits could have been prevented if the pastors or the staff members would have operated in this gift. Remember that the enemy will use people and cause them to do things that are ungodly and unscriptural. Most of these people aren't demon possessed or even meaning to harm. They most likely think that they are doing God a favor. But God can show us how the enemy would want to use these well-meaning people.

As far as seeing in the spirit, there is a difference between discerning of spirits and spiritual discernment. Discerning of spirits is the ability to see in the spirit through your mind's eye. Spiritual discernment is when your natural eyes are open to the spirit world. Whenever you see something in the spirit with your natural eyes, it is processed through your natural faculties, and most of the time, is very difficult to handle. When I was first saved, I asked the Lord to give me spiritual discernment. Then one day, the Lord opened my natural eyes to see what was only supposed to be seen by my spirit man. I saw a demon right in front of me. As soon as I saw it, my spirit man rose up, and I rebuked it in the name of the Lord. Immediately, the Holy Spirit said, "Be careful what you pray for, you may get something that you really don't want." He then taught me the difference between the two. We should never be afraid of the devil, yet the things of the spirit are much easier to handle when your spirit discerns it.

A TOTAL CHANGE

We have ministered to people who have problems in their lives that have hindered them and their family members for years. The Lord often gives us insight into the source of these problems. For instance, I was praying for a young girl at a youth rally, and the Lord showed me that her family was under a curse of witchcraft that stemmed from a prior generation.

It manifested itself in the form of fear and anxiety. I saw her mother and an older woman standing next to her and sensed that the curse came though her mother's family. I said to her, "Your mother is under the influence of witchcraft because of someone in her background. That spirit of witchcraft has been coming against your family and has caused oppression and depression in the following generations as well." Later, her mother came to the meeting and confirmed even the setting and place that I saw in the vision. The Lord gave discernment into the cause and gave the power to break the curse.

This family had been suffering from these problems but didn't have an understanding of the cause. They never realized that a family member who lived in the hills practiced occult things long ago and that it would have an effect on their lives generations later. But God did, and He was kind enough to reveal the spirit behind it so that they could be free. The girl approached me at another meeting and told me that she and her family have totally changed. Their lives were changed because we took hold of that dirty, lying spirit when God gave the discernment, and broke the power of it.

I remember an instance when I first got saved and we were praying outside in front of my friend's house. We had a group of people show up for the prayer meeting and we were not ashamed of the gospel. But unknown to me, one of my friends was afraid that his parents would be looking out the window and see us praying on their front lawn. I heard the voice of God say to me, "In his heart, he is afraid of his parents looking out, and they would be ashamed of him." God allowed me to know what was in his heart so that I could encourage him to stay focused on the Lord. In the New Testament, we see Jesus do this many times. Jesus said that He perceived what was in their hearts. Not only did He know what was in their hearts; He knew who was with Him and who was not. He knew these things by the gift of discerning of spirits.

The Holy Spirit is willing to use anyone who makes themselves available and has a desire to use this gift for God's glory and not for personal gain. This gift will enable you to see what spirits are operating and controlling people and to discern the motivations behind their actions.

> Now it happened on another Sabbath, also, that He entered the synagogue and taught. And a man was there whose right hand was withered. So the scribes and Pharisees watched Him closely, whether He would heal on the Sabbath, that they might find an accusation against Him. But He knew their thoughts, and said to the man who had the withered hand, "Arise and stand here." And he arose and stood.
>
> Luke 6:6-8, NKJV

Jesus discerned that the Pharisees were trying to find fault in Him. Instead of giving into their pressure, He used the revelation to make them even more upset in order to destroy the control that they were trying to bind Him under. This gift is awesome for breaking controlling spirits and/or the influence of controlling people.

KNOWN BY THE FRUIT

This gift is often in action when someone walks into the room and you suddenly have a good or bad feeling or impression of them. I believe that the fruit of the spirit will cooperate with the discerning of spirits. Peace, love, and joy are just a few that will keep you in check. Even though you might feel uncomfortable with someone or something in your emotions, the fruit of the Spirit will help clarify whether it is your flesh or your spirit. Your carnal nature might cause you not to love someone that you feel uncomfortable about, almost as if it is a personal thing.

With spiritual discernment, you should be able to continue to love them.

If you discern that someone has his or her own agenda, it is best not to say anything when you are first learning to use this gift, just take it to prayer. We tend to put more trust in our ability to confront than God's ability to change someone through prayer. Pray and watch for the outcome. It won't take long for their agenda to surface if you are praying. Never, ever try to control someone's will through prayer because you think that you have discerned something. Just ask God to change their motives if they are impure.

Ministers, the Lord has placed someone in your life who has discerning spirit grace to protect you from trouble. It could be your spouse or a staff member. You would be doing yourself and your ministries a grave injustice if you take them for granted and not take what they're saying seriously enough to pray about it. If you're the person that God has trusted with this gift, seek God to know about good things and not only the negative. It is much easier for humans to pick up the negative before the positive. The last thing you want is to become judgmental. Don't just go around judging everyone because of every little feeling you get. When you get a feeling, just spend extra time praying; let God confirm it several times before you approach the person involved.

There are many more angels than demons; it's a shame that we are always looking for the devil and not for God. God is opening the eyes of believers to see angels in these last days to encourage us that there are more of us than there are of them.

Many intercessors have been led astray to think that if they have the gift of discerning of spirits then they are actually prophets or prophetesses. God may be giving them discernment into what is happening in the church for prayer's sake. Instead of praying, they organize a meeting with the pastor to tell him how to run the church and what changes he needs to make to get back into the will of God. If you are not anointed to speak the prophetic word, it will be powerless and end up causing more trouble than help. If you're anointed to pray, the power of God will only move when you pray, and the changes will only come through prayer.

MOCKING SPIRITS

> Now it happened, as we went to prayer, that a certain slave girl possessed with a spirit of divination met us, who brought her masters much profit by fortune-telling. This girl followed Paul and us, and cried out, saying, "These men are the servants of the Most High God, who proclaim to us the way of salvation." And this she did for many days. But Paul, greatly annoyed, turned and said to the spirit, "I command you in the name of Jesus Christ to come out of her." And he came out that very hour.
>
> Acts 16:16-18, NKJV

This girl was actually telling the truth and announcing a great confirmation to the people. If we look at this just at its face value, it looks as if there was nothing wrong with what she was doing. When in all actuality, she was bound by a mocking spirit, which was causing unnecessary attention to Paul and the others. Paul sensed that the flattery from this girl was wrong, the gift of discerning of spirits kicked in, and he knew that this was false praise. Being grieved by the demon controlling the girl, Paul moved into the gift of faith and commanded the evil spirit to leave her. Once again, we see another gift coming into operation to assist in the work: first revelation, then power.

We need this gift in the church. Many people come with flattering and encouraging words, but their hearts are evil. If you are naturally minded and can't discern what spirit these people are operating under, it could be very dangerous. It might sound nice, but the word will have some type of seduction about it that will cause the Christlikeness in you to feel uncomfortable.

> And in Lystra a certain man without strength in his feet was sitting, a cripple from his mother's womb, who had never walked. *This* man heard Paul speaking. Paul, observing him intently and seeing that he had faith to be healed, said with a loud voice, "Stand up straight on your feet!" And he leaped and walked.
>
> Acts 14:8-10, NKJV

How could Paul know that this man had the faith to be healed? Paul could see the man's faith through the discerning of spirits. There is no knowledge of what Paul was preaching, but it was enough for this man to believe. The reason that most churches don't have supernatural occurrences is because they don't build the people's faith to expect the supernatural. This man's faith was so strong that the Holy Ghost was excited about it. God anointed Paul to see the faith in the man's heart, and then God anointed him with healing virtue to meet the man's faith.

FALSE PROPHETS

This gift also helps us discern when something is not birthed of God and when someone is under the unction of the Holy Ghost. Too often, we say that it is not God when God is moving. We are living in the days that Jesus spoke of when there would be false teachers and false prophets. All we really need to follow after are the true teachers and prophets, because as long as we find the truth, we don't have to be concerned with the false. What happens when you see those psychic commercials? You are grieved if the Holy Spirit is in you. Are any of you compelled to call? No! That is because the Spirit of God is inside of you and He gives discernment of what is right and what is wrong. Although, when you are in need and a man of God tells you to call an 800 number for prayer, you will not hesitate to call. You are discerning the difference between the two. Do not make it too difficult. You are discerning what is God and what is not. It does run deeper than those examples, but if you can't discern in the small, you sure will miss the more complicated matters. God is raising up a generation of Christians who will operate in all the gifts of God so that the world can be reached.

REVELATION GIFTS:
PRACTICAL APPLICATION

RECOGNITION:

Recognize these gifts by the desires of your heart. The Lord allows us to have a desire for the things of God, then He leads us and teaches us how to fulfill these desires. Some gifts will be easier to operate in because of your natural inclination, personality, and your motivational and/or five-fold gifting. The understanding in this is to go after what comes easiest to you. If it's easy to prophesy and you desire to pray for the sick, step into the prophetic and study healing. Soon they both will be operating strongly in your life. Lastly, you can recognize your gifts by what urge you have when the anointing comes upon you. What happens when you feel the anointing? For the revelation gifts, you may experience clarity in mind, a feeling of knowing something very strongly, or visions may flash in front of you. You may even tend to daydream and find yourself watching an open vision, as if it were a movie, as you see into the spirit world.

OPERATION:

Be willing to approach anyone when the Lord leads, be willing to pray when the Lord leads, and be willing to hold your peace until the Lord leads you to speak. Remember that most of the time the gifts of revelation will not operate alone, they will activate another gift, causing a reaction in you, the recipient, or the power of God to bring about the miracle. In stepping out in faith, always be wise, gracious, and loving.

DEVELOPMENT:

There are three things that we can do to activate these revelation gifts. Ask God to use you and to give you revelation, believe that He will use you, and step out in faith as you recognize His leading. The best way to train your ear and intuition to the gifts of revelation is in intercession. When we approach God on the behalf of someone else, God sees a selfless heart and begins to show us what to pray for through the use of these gifts. I believe that within a thirty-minute time span of intercession, any person will operate in at least one, if not all, of the gifts of revelation. If you can't minister to people in prayer for half an hour, how can the Lord use you on the street where there are distractions all around?

Learn in private, then allow God to interrupt you in public. The best way to develop these gifts is by communion with the Holy Spirit. Just spend time listening to Him. If at first you don't notice a difference, continue listening. The Holy Spirit wants to know that you want to know Him and not just receive His gifts. Spend time building trust, and in due time, you will find yourself conversing with the third Person of the Godhead. Once you hear His voice in this way, you will be able to hear His voice in ministering.

Another good way to develop your gift is to pray while someone that operates in these gifts is ministering. I would watch the "This is Your Day" program, and as soon as Benny Hinn started praying for the sick with the words of knowledge, I would ask the Holy Spirit to give me the same words. At first, I was completely wrong, but after some time, I started getting more and more accurate.

One day, I was watching television and the Lord spoke to me and told me to go to the bowling alley. After a time of arguing, I decided to go. I believe the Lord knew that I would argue for at least thirty minutes, so he told me thirty minutes ahead of time. When I got to the bowling alley, the Lord showed me who to talk to. I was very nervous, so I just walked around and played video games, hoping that this fellow would leave. This guy was on a date and the Lord wanted me to tell him something. I just imagined how I would feel if someone gave me a word from God out of the blue. That is a little weird; that's why the Lord does not ask for our opinion, He just wants us to obey. I saw them preparing to leave, so I went outside and waited for them. When he came out, I hit him with the Word of the Lord, and he was wonderfully ministered to. But before I could give him the word, I needed to get off my couch.

Don't ever stop training your gift. I watch William Branham's videos all the time because I want more. Lastly, spend time listening instead of always talking, and pull out your Bible and study, meditating on the word of God. As you are trustworthy with little, God will trust you with more!

CHAPTER 9

THE GIFTS OF POWER

To another faith by the same Spirit, to another gifts of healings by the same Spirit, to another the working of miracles.

1 Corinthians 12:9-10, NKJV

While studying the book of Acts, I noticed that every other book in the New Testament had a closing statement that ended it. The book of Acts is open-ended. I realized that the book of Acts is the beginning documentation of the start of the Church, and there is not a classic writer's sign off because the volume is still being written through our lives and acts. The power that we see in Acts should be just as evident in our lives. Actually, the Bible makes it clear that we should walk in the same power that Jesus ministered in.

Most assuredly, I say to you, he who believes in Me, the works that I do he will do also; and greater *works* than these he will do, because I go to My Father.

John 14:12, NKJV

Many believe this means that the church as a *whole* would do greater works, not necessarily individuals. That theory doesn't make sense, because since my conversion I have seen the works of Jesus, as well as the greater works. We have seen many people healed and set free. We have seen people set free from the oppressions of the devil. I am persuaded that we can walk with the Holy Spirit without measure if we are taught by Him.

IN YOUR FOOTSTEPS, LORD

Right from the start, I made up my mind to see the same things that the Apostles experienced. I would start each day by praying for the Lord to use me as He used the Apostles. My prayer was, "I will go on the streets, use me to touch others, minister through me, do whatever You want with me, I am Yours!" Then the Lord led me to start riding the bus to a nearby city to witness on the street; it would take me an hour and a half to get there. The Lord would start moving before I reached the downtown area. I would read my Bible all the way. I asked the Lord to send me someone that I could share the gospel with. Then, suddenly, a passenger on the bus would sit right next to me and they would ask how I was doing, and that was my open door.

As I rode the bus, I was able to lead people to the Lord and soon began to pray for people to be healed. I would introduce myself as a Christian, thinking that it would give me instant credibility. Little did I know that it would turn most of them off. It did not discourage me; I was looking for the one individual who was open and ready. I remember praying for an elderly lady on the bus wearing hearing aids. I approached her to ask if I could pray for her. She replied yes and confessed to being a Christian also. I put my fingers in her ears. I could see everyone around us getting very uncomfortable. This also didn't bother me; I was too focused on seeing the power of God. I said, "In the Name of Jesus, I command these ears to hear!" I did the same thing that I saw Benny Hinn do. This was all that I knew to do. I was just a few months old in the Lord. Paul started preaching almost immediately after he was saved. When I was done praying, the lady thanked me, then put her hearing aids back in her ears and went her way. I went back home very upset by this undeniable shame and disappointment. However, I had faith; an unmovable faith. I said "God, You are either God or a liar!" (This is not my advice to you. In my ignorance, I spoke very foolishly to the Almighty, but He looked at my heart not my ignorance. What love!)

FIRST DISAPPOINTMENTS

You see, I had thrown Christianity out of my life at an early age. By the age of thirteen, I professed to be an atheist. I was devastated by the death of my first best friend, my grandfather. I remember for many years, falling on my knees between the ages of 7 to 11, as he was on his sickbed and dying, asking God to heal him from cancer. I was calling on God to do something the traditional church that my family attended at the time didn't teach. But I believed that if God could create, He could also fix things. My grandfather eventually died, but not before he was wonderfully saved. Yet, salvation wasn't what I wanted. I wanted to be able to talk to my best friend. This was a major blow to my faith. With this disappointment in my heart, I left my grandmother, who used to take me to church, to live with my mother, who was a Muslim. The God of the Bible disappointed me, and shortly after, I realized that the god of the Koran was equally disappointing because he never answered me. So,

I threw God out of my life altogether. Of course, the Lord later changed my mind and is using that very experience as a motivation to destroy the works of the devil as often as possible!

ZEAL WITHOUT KNOWLEDGE

When I returned to my house disappointed after ministering on the streets, I went into my room to confront the Creator of the universe. I was speaking as a young man who had been looking for the Truth all his life. And I wasn't about to commit to a lying God. So, I said, "You are either the God that I read about in the Bible or not. I will not serve You if You're a liar. I will go back to what I know."

The devil had already tried to recruit me and promised to give me power. I knew the devil would give me power, and when he was tired of using me, he would try to kill me. I truly didn't want to go that route, so I said God, "If You are the true God, if You are the One the Bible says that You are, You will start using me, and I will serve You all my life." We have to have that type of fight in us, that type of determination. Not that you talk to God that way. No, He is not our servant. We are His children, submitted to Him. I was just fresh from the streets. I did not have enough sense to know that I should have a fear (reverence) of God. Yet, I think that God liked my boldness; He saw my stupidity and said, "I could use this guy." God wanted His Truth shared and all I wanted was the Truth. This was truly a match made in Heaven. Do you want the Truth enough to keep pressing on until you see the God of Elijah? This generation has the heart of Elisha; we are looking for the God who moved the Red Sea. We are looking for the God of Elijah.

NO ONE GOT HEALED

After going through all of this, I would go back out to preach and pray for the sick. My goal was to see someone rise out of a wheelchair before my sixth month anniversary of being born again. That was what drove me. I separated myself to pray, read, and seek God. My grandmother (I lived with her), would call me for dinner or to answer the phone, but I asked her not to disturb me while I was praying to God. Then, looking for someone to minister to, I would go to the city again. I prayed for many people and they still didn't get healed. I would go through the same process again and again. I would go back to my room and cry out to God again saying, "I will not give up until You move. I will not quit until I know that You are true or false. I am not going to stop until You heal them and if You do not, I am walking!"

I have been a Muslim, an atheist, and then some. I wanted to know if He was true. I was relentless. I did not see any results. Some people have immediate results, but I did not. I kept going because I fell in love with the presence of the Lord. I already loved Him. I remembered how I felt when I got saved. It was like liquid love running through me, cleansing me from my guilt and shame. I said, "If this is a lie like all the others, I do not know what I am going to do." So, I held on. You have got to hold on and keep on pressing on.

POWER AND PEANUT BUTTER

Finally, one day as I was in the kitchen at a friend's house making a peanut butter sandwich, another one of our friends came over. She walked into the kitchen and said she had a headache. Jokingly, I lifted my hand and put it to her forehead and said, "In the Name of Jesus be healed." She fell to the floor under the power of God. When she got up, she said she felt as if she had a hole in her head and the headache was completely gone. I was rejoicing. Finally, there was power!

I believe that God saw how hungry I was, and I sure was hungry by this time. We immediately invited all of our friends over to have a prayer meeting on the lawn. We saw people's legs grow out and other miracles right there in the front yard. All of the miracles I had been waiting and pressing into God for started happening as people went under the power of God. I was faithful in little, which caused God to bring the increase. More than we understand, the Lord truly wants us to touch people.

A LOVING PASTOR

There were many signs and wonders, people falling under the power of God and being delivered. The first real miracle was undocumented, a young boy who was deaf from birth. After praying for him, he could hear. I was very excited because this was similar to the first miracle that I had seen on Benny Hinn's television show. But the miracles and dramatic healings were sporadic. I wanted to see people's lives changed. From then on, things got worse for me because I left the streets and started ministering in my church. I had just started going to a new church and was very aggressive and zealous. My pastor would preach a great sermon and then call the people to respond to an altar call. When the people started forward to the altars, the anointing fell on me and my hands started tingling. So instead of finding someone in the crowd sitting next to me to minister to, I assumed that the Lord wanted me to take over the altar call by praying for the people. The Pastor did not know me. I was new to this church. (Please don't do this in your church.) I ran to the front and started from one end and laid hands on about fifty people, they all fell out under the power of God. The pastor was such a lovely person; he let me do it the first time only because the Lord told him not to stop me. Fortunately for me, he was very sensitive to the Holy Spirit to obey the voice of God.

The next week I did the same thing. This pastor still didn't feel released from God to stop me. Many other pastors would have stopped what God was trying to develop in me. Obeying God was more important than his reputation. The third time, he said, "Tracey, that is enough." Later he called me to his office and told me why he didn't stop me at first. He said that he wanted to invest in me and to teach me about what I was operating in. He started sharing with me what was orderly and what was out of order. He put me in classes to learn more about leading people to the Lord and seeing them filled with the Holy Spirit. He also put me on the altar worker's prayer team. He didn't squash my gifts; he gave me room to develop. My pastor never stopped me, but the older Christians in the church started arguing and questioning my motives.

You will make mistakes and some people might not get healed, but the fact is, most Christians in the body of Christ are unwilling to take those kinds of risks. The brunt of your persecution will come from people who most likely mean well but just don't understand. Don't react to them by arguing and throwing the spear back at them. Keep a sharp edge on your gift by continuing your ministry wherever you are, and pray for the Church. Lord willing, you will have a pastor like I did.

If you are a pastor reading this book, I will encourage you with a little wisdom from my personal experience. The people you sincerely invest in and seek to develop beyond your vision will, in turn, help your vision and be forever loyal to you. People can tell whether you care about them or whether you just want to use them. It's wonderful to find someone who is willing to take of their time and get involved. A moving car can be steered; a parked car is impossible to steer. Steer rather than stop.

PURPOSE OF POWER

The gifts of power are for the purpose of releasing God's power to man on the behalf of God, resulting in spiritual and natural breakthroughs, for the sole purpose of defusing and destroying the works of the devil.

CHAPTER 10

THE GIFT OF FAITH

To another faith by the same Spirit.

1 Corinthians 12:9, NKJV

The gift of faith is the supernatural ability to believe God without human doubt, unbelief, or reasoning. The gift of faith is an extension of the measure of faith that has been delivered to every believer. When this gift kicks in, you have faith to believe for unimaginable things. The gift of faith has the ability to supersede natural and supernatural laws. It will give you the immovable faith to move whatever mountain God is leading you to confront, as well as give you the confidence to draw from the spirit-realm into the natural. We need this type of faith to believe God for nations to be opened to the gospel.

> By faith we understand that the worlds were framed by
> the word of God, so that the things which are seen were
> not made of things which are visible.
>
> Hebrews 11:3, NKJV

This gift of faith will cause us to speak the things that are not as if they are, causing them to manifest through the power of prayer and declaration. The gift of faith cannot be worked up. The Holy Spirit, for the purpose of God, delivers it to us.

> And seeing a fig tree by the road, He came to it and
> found nothing on it but leaves, and said to it, "'Let no
> fruit grow on you ever again." Immediately the fig tree
> withered away. And when the disciples saw *it*, they mar-
> veled, saying, "How did the fig tree wither away so soon?"
>
> Matthew 21:19-20, NKJV

ABSOLUTE FAITH

This gift of faith is synonymous with the gift of assurance. The gift of assurance doesn't give any room for doubt whatsoever. Jesus spoke to the fig tree, commanding it to obey His absolute faith. Absolute faith will not allow nature, demons, or fear to resist it. We speak in the Name of Jesus and everything around submits. I have prayed for sick people, under the gift of faith, when they didn't have the faith to believe God themselves for their healing. As I prayed, a doubtless confidence hit my soul and they were healed. It was as if they borrowed the faith that the Lord delivered to me for their healing. I want to make it clear that I didn't pray against their will, they were willing; they just didn't have enough faith to believe they could receive.

The gift of faith is the only gift where the people to whom you are ministering will acquire faith from the giver in order to receive their needed ministry. Although the gift of faith is not the *substance of things hoped for* that makes the body whole, it is the confidence that activates the gift of healing. When T.L. Osborn preached to the unsaved in a third world country, the gift of faith activated people to believe for what he preached. This is the very reason a person hearing of the saving and healing power of Jesus will receive just that. The gift of faith will enable the gift of prophecy to dig deeper into the lives and future of people. Romans 12:6 encourages us to prophesy according to our faith. This faith is the power that activates the seemingly impossible in our lives.

The gift of faith is powerful but cannot override the will of a human being. God Himself would never override the moral obligation of man. In the same way, His gifts will not. As the fig tree withered, it caused the disciples to marvel. The gift of faith is a marvelous gift. It truly shows God as the God of the impossible. The other thing that we can see in this scripture is that they marveled at the speedy obedience of the withered tree.

The gift of faith withered this tree. In verse 21, Jesus assured the disciples that if they had faith as a mustard seed, then they could move a mountain. All we need is a portion of this faith that comes as a gift from God. We have a mustard seed of faith without the gift. The mustard seed is one of the smallest seeds there is. You and I can move a mountain with that amount of faith. We all have that much faith. Now, when the gift of faith hits us, how many mountains can we move? I know, at some time, the gift of faith has come upon you. There is a time when you experienced a faith where you said, "I do not care what the circumstances are; I am about to get a breakthrough." You may have become very angry at the obstacle in your path and shouted at it and, surprisingly, the challenge moved. This is the gift of faith.

Another notable thought regarding the mustard seed is that seeds grow into reproductive trees or plants. The smallest seed in the world can reproduce. Even the smallest faith in the world reproduces of its kind.

RIGHTEOUS ANGER

One day, a lady came to me with a fibroid tumor the size of a large orange. She informed me that she was scheduled for surgery the following Tuesday. I laid my hands on her forehead to pray for her. I wasn't persuaded that she would be healed. I prayed a prayer of faith in the Name of Jesus, hoping that the woman would have the faith to pull on God. As I looked into her face, I saw the tears streaming and her lips were grasping for any help from the Lord. I prayed, "Father, in the Name of Jesus, I ask that You would heal this woman and set her free." Then something hit me; a supernatural, incredible faith came out of nowhere. God put His supernatural faith in me that this woman would walk out completely healed.

When the gift of faith hits, all asking stops, and the commanding starts. The gift of faith commands with the same creative power as the Father commanded the earth and the universe to exist. So, I said, "In the Name of Jesus, GO!" She went down to the floor under the power of God. She was unaware of the effect of the prayer.

She went to the doctor the following Tuesday. She requested the doctor to check her before they went in to remove the tumor. They optically searched for the growth and found only some scar tissue, which they removed that day. Thank you, Jesus, for your power to change lives! The life of God caused the life in the tumor to wither away. God completely healed her and showed His love. I did not have the faith for her to be healed at first, but God desired to heal her, so He gave me the faith necessary to bring about the miracle.

UNSAVED AND HEALED

Years ago, I had the opportunity to minister several times to a substance abuse support group, which met at the church that I attended. In this group was a man who suffered with heart problems. The Lord released a word of knowledge in one of the meetings, revealing this man's problem. The gift of faith hit me after the word of knowledge was received. I tapped him in the chest and said, "In the Name of Jesus be healed." A few weeks later, he came to the meeting and told me that his heart was completely healed. Three weeks after that, he came to me again and told me that he got saved that day. He got saved after he was healed. Most unsaved people are willing to take a chance on being healed and often will get healed easier than Christians. The gift of faith will cause you to do things before you even have a chance to reason them away. When this happens, there is no chance for you to doubt or be afraid.

PRAYER OF FAITH OR GIFT OF FAITH?

And fixing his eyes on him, with John, Peter said, "Look at us." So he gave them his attention, expecting to receive something from them. Then Peter said, "Silver and gold I do not have, but what I do have I give you: In the name of Jesus Christ of Nazareth, rise up and walk." And he took him by the right hand and lifted *him* up, and immediately his feet and anklebones received strength.

Acts 3:4-7, NKJV

The gift of faith hit Peter so fast that the man did not have a chance to decide not to receive. Instantly, the lame man was healed. The Holy Spirit supernaturally distributes this gift of faith, which is different than the prayer of faith. This is a prayer that any believer can pray at any given time. There is a great difference between the two. James 5 says that if there are any sick among you, the prayer of faith shall make them whole.

It is not based upon anointing, but a mustard seed faith. Once the gift of faith kicks in, you do not pray for a need to be fulfilled, you command it to be fulfilled.

Smith Wigglesworth operated strongly in the gift of faith. If you ever had the chance to sit under his ministry, you would have seen people healed by a fist blow to whatever part of the body that was ailing them. So, if you suffered with a stomachache, he might punch you in the stomach to release healing to you. Of course, this wasn't the only way that he ministered, but this did occur while he was operating under the gift of faith.

Under the gift of faith, people do wild things. This is very true in this story of Peter ministering to the lame man. With complete boldness, he pulled the man to his feet. The man rose immediately, according to the faith that was delivered to Peter.

STRANGE METHODS

Another such account is when Jesus healed a blind man in a shocking manner. We hear, very often, of some pastor or leader getting upset at a method of an evangelist or a supernatural minister. Usually, the reason is because many people try to reason away the moving of the Holy Spirit. Although the Holy Spirit is pragmatic, He often calls for unfamiliar methods to achieve His goal. He is not subject to operating within the limitations of human logic. This is why, for so many years, the church has turned its back on the prophetic and apostolic ministries. Both the prophetic and apostolic ministry operate strongly within the realms of the spirit, in order to establish true spiritual government. The gift of faith is a function of authority and power.

"A RUSHING MIGHTY WIND"

Look at how bizarrely this miracle came to pass. When I first started praying for people, they would go down under the power of God, then some "older and more mature" people started to say that I was pushing people over. Well, this was silly to me because, first of all, I knew that God didn't need me to push people over, and secondly, people can get healed just as wonderfully standing up. Seeing that I hate religion, I asked the Lord to anoint me to blow on people so that I could stand some distance away from the people and He could be seen touching them. Weeks went by and I had forgotten about this prayer.

As I was praying for a group of people, a burning started in my chest and increased until I began to breathe a little heavily. Then I heard the Holy Spirit say, "A rushing mighty wind, and no one can stand in the Presence of an awesome God." I didn't understand what He said at first, but I soon grasped that He was releasing me to breathe on people. So I did, and people began to get healed that way. Individuals started falling under the power of God by one breath. This stopped the religious accusations for a short while. We forget that Jesus is not religious, and He wants to destroy all false beliefs. This was the gift of faith in operation. Since then, people have received breakthroughs through shaking hands, running, counting, clapping, and even snapping fingers.

Remember when it was considered uncivilized to snap your fingers? Now God uses it to touch people. I think I'll start handing gum out in church services so that God can touch His people. In numerous, odd ways, God has moved, and I think He likes it that way. There are many uses for the gift of faith. The gift of faith casts out demons, heals the sick, and brings divine confidence for anything that a person can believe for, causing it to come into being according to the will of God, even to the point of raising the dead.

> Now on the first *day* of the week, when the disciples came together to break bread, Paul, ready to depart the next day, spoke to them and continued his message until

midnight. There were many lamps in the upper room where they were gathered together. And in a window sat a certain young man named Eutychus, who was sinking into a deep sleep. He was overcome by sleep; and as Paul continued speaking, he fell down from the third story and was taken up dead. But Paul went down, fell on him, and embracing *him* said, "Do not trouble yourselves, for his life is in him." Now when he had come up, had broken bread and eaten, and talked a long while, even till daybreak, he departed. And they brought the young man in alive, and they were not a little comforted.

Acts 20:7-12, NKJV

GIFT OF CONFIDENCE

This is a great example of a young man brought back to life by the gift of faith. Eutychus fell out of a window and was found dead. Paul approached the young man's dead body and he spoke out the words, "Do not trouble yourselves, for his life is in him." The boy didn't immediately rise to his feet and go on with life. Paul spoke these words and left the lifeless body where it laid and went to have something to eat. It even says that Paul had broken bread and talked for a long time before the young man came up. Who knows when this young man came in, but it was obvious that it was quite some time after Paul left. Can you imagine the reaction of the people? Paul fell on him, embraced him, spoke a few words, and then left. I'm sure many of the believers around were wondering what this fellow was doing. Had Paul given up? No, Paul was so confident that he just walked off, knowing that the work had been done and that it had to manifest sooner or later. To bring true understanding to the gift of faith is to translate it as the gift of confidence. Such supernatural confidence that supersedes any doubt that may have been in the crowd.

When the anointing for faith arises, you will have a supernatural confidence that whatever you ask in prayer, as long as you believe, it will be delivered to you. This anointing may manifest tangibly, yet for the most part, it is a conviction in the soul that demands a response to your words.

The gift of faith seems as if it is simply a gift that enhances other gifts, but in actuality, it is a gift that enables the other gifts to work at their full potential. The lack of faith can keep us from operating in our gifts with great power, and a gift operated under faith is the only way to be able to correctly walk in the fullness of a gift. After all, without faith, it is impossible to please God. Another way to say this is, "Without confidence in God and His abilities, it is impossible to please God." Faith is the confidence that creates. The gift of faith releases creative power. Creative miracles are wrought by the gift of faith. The worlds were created by faith. The gift of faith has the ability to see into the future and to create what it sees through a spoken word. The gift of faith will cause life to come from death. The gift of faith does not ask whether or not it is finished, it knows that it is finished.

CHAPTER 11

THE GIFTS OF HEALINGS

To another gifts of healings by the same Spirit.

1 Corinthians 12:9, NKJV

FAITH TO HEAL

The gifts of healings is supernatural power to heal all manner of sickness without human aid or medicine. This gift comes through the anointing. Some ministers operate in the gifts of healings. In their meetings or crusades, there is an atmosphere or presence for healing. My wife, Nathalie, operates in the gifts of healings and has seen many healed under her hands. As we reflected on the miracles and healings while writing this book, she described an exciting miracle that had taken place a few years back.

She was praying for a lady who had been through several surgeries that left her with a severely damaged knee. Certain parts in her knee had been removed to the point that it was impossible for her to bend or kneel on her right knee. There was continual pain so that she could not sleep at night without taking strong pain pills. As Nathalie laid her hands on the woman's knee, boldness for a miracle came upon her. Under Nathalie's hands, the sound of cracking bone was heard, and her knee was instantly restored. She quickly tested it by having the lady bend and rest on the healed knee. The wonderful Miracle Worker put in brand new bone and cartilage! The woman was so overjoyed that she asked if she could accept Jesus as her Lord and Savior as well. The power of God is the proof of a living Christ to bring people to Jesus. No matter what the need is, God has given us the power to meet the needs of the lost and hurting.

There is an anointing available for strictly healing the sick. The gifts of healings work differently than the other gifts of power, in that it has one sole purpose: to restore to health that which is sick. Healing can manifest instantly as a miracle, or it can take a period of time. The gifts of healings are not isolated to physical illnesses. The gifts of healings cure any ailments: body, emotional, mental, and even financial. It is described as the gifts of healings for this purpose. The Holy Spirit, depending on what He can trust you with, distributes the different gifts of healings.

> Then He appointed twelve, that they might be with Him and that He might send them out to preach, and to have power to heal sicknesses and to cast out demons.
> Mark 3:14-15, NKJV

This clearly states that the Lord gave power to the disciples to heal illnesses. It doesn't say some illnesses. It would be unscriptural for us to assume that God would distribute to his followers something less than what He, Himself, would operate in if He expects us to accomplish greater things than He accomplished here on the earth.

> And these signs will follow those who believe: In My name they will cast out demons; they will speak with new tongues; they will take up serpents; and if they drink anything deadly, it will by no means hurt them; they will lay hands on the sick, and they will recover.
>
> Mark 16:17-18, NKJV

ANOINTED FOR A REASON

The Lord will use any believer to heal the sick. Through God's promises, we as believers have authority to cure the sick. Every Christian should pray for the sick, but not everyone is to make it his or her entire ministry in life. The anointing only comes for ministry. This is also true for the anointing that activates the gifts of healings. This unction comes from the initiation of the Holy Spirit, not only by our reasoning of the truth that is found in the Word of God. People with this ministry will always be more aware of sick people around them than other believers. They are always looking for the opportunity to destroy this oppression of the devil.

> So He Himself *often* withdrew into the wilderness and prayed. Now it happened on a certain day, as He was teaching, that there were Pharisees and teachers of the law sitting by, who had come out of every town of Galilee, Judea, and Jerusalem. And the power of the Lord was *present* to heal them. Then behold, men brought on a bed a man who was paralyzed, whom they sought to bring in and lay before Him. And when they could not

find how they might bring him in, because of the crowd, they went up on the housetop and let him down with *his* bed through the tiling into the midst before Jesus. When He saw their faith, He said to him, "Man, your sins are forgiven you."

Luke 5:16-20, NKJV

WHAT'S THE SECRET?

There are several very important points in this passage of scripture that will give us an understanding of why the power of the Lord was present and why the man was healed. The first point we find in verse 16; Jesus separated Himself often to pray. This was a key factor in the life and ministry of Jesus. Between His times of prayer, He walked through life working miracles. You must be prepared to pray if you want the power to change lives.

Secondly, in verse 17, we see that Jesus was teaching. One thing that I have learned is that you must teach on the blessing that you want the people to receive. If you desire for God to use you in healing, then talk about healing. If you want God to work miracles, then talk about miracles. If you want people to get saved, then talk about salvation. The same goes with financial increase. What you teach or talk about is what you get! I have seen this in action with many ministers, including in our own ministry. This principle is not confined to the five-fold ministry. One-on-one ministry is one of the most effective forms of touching a person's life. It is simple to teach on the benefits of salvation; it's as simple as telling your testimony. Your testimony being how your life was without Christ, how you met Christ, and what your life has been like ever since. Everyone should be able to share their testimony within sixty seconds.

CREATE EXPECTATION

Prayer and teaching on salvation activated the power of the Lord being present to heal. Please understand that I am not describing a formula. These are principles and lifestyles that bring a reward when practically applied. The key is that whatever you sow, you reap. At this point, we notice the sick looking for Jesus. Once you start teaching about healing, whether you have been used in this type of ministry before or not, people will approach you with the expectation to receive their healing. The greatest things that I have noticed in meetings conducted by men of God like Reinhard Bonnke, Benny Hinn, and T.L. Osborn is that there is a great expectation built up to receive. The faith bank is high. In verse 20, Jesus saw the faith of the man to receive his healing. Believe me, it is much easier to work with faith than it is to work with doubt.

Thirdly, work with the faith of the receiver. They must understand that their faith is important in receiving their healing, just as your faith is instrumental in helping them receive. For this reason, your teaching will be very important, especially for a Christian. Based on my experience, I believe that non-believers are easier to minister healing to because most of them don't have any religious doctrines to overcome that tell them they can't receive from God. Which brings us to the next point: Jesus healed this man by forgiving his sins. If we can cause Christians to understand that with the receiving of Jesus comes salvation for spirit, soul, and body, then we can destroy guilt, shame, unbelief, religion, and tradition, which are major obstacles to receiving healing.

> Surely He has borne our griefs and carried our sorrows; yet we esteemed Him stricken, smitten by God, and afflicted. But He *was* wounded for our transgressions, *He was* bruised for our iniquities; the chastisement

for our peace was upon Him, and by His stripes we
are healed.

Isaiah 53:4-5, NKJV

FREEDOM IN YOUR BODY

These verses are very important to believers. This version says that He has borne our griefs. The Hebrew word for griefs is *choliy* (khol-ee'), which means malady, anxiety, and calamity. Jesus has taken these things from us. This is the true life insurance policy from Heaven. Every physical sickness is covered with this policy. The wonderful thing is that there is not even a deductible; the deductible has already been paid!

FREEDOM IN YOUR SOUL

Then it says that Jesus has carried our sorrows, has taken on the burden, and has completely removed the yoke of sorrows off of our backs. The word "sorrow" in the Hebrew is *mak'ob* (mak-obe'), which means anguish. This is dealing with the realms of our soul. Again, this is covered under the same policy, without a deductible. This covers any affliction that deals with the mind, will, and emotions. Our soul can receive a free overhaul through the power of God. This includes Alzheimer's, insanity, mental anxiety, schizophrenia, depression, oppression, possession, paranoia, and any other lie of the devil.

Verse 5 says, "He was wounded for our transgressions." The word "transgression" here is *pesha* (peh'-shah), a revolt, rebellion, sin, transgression, or trespass. The word "iniquity" is *avon* (aw-vone'); perversity, i.e. (moral) evil. This scripture is dealing with the spirit of man and gives us a solution to be free from the spiritual ills that we have sown or that the devil has trapped us and our forefathers by. It promises us eternal salvation, the right to walk with Jesus in eternity. This salvation awakens the dead spirit of man and joins it to the life of the Holy Spirit forevermore.

This takes care of past, present, or future sins against God's nature and will. Now that we are joined to the Master, we need the policy to keep us connected. This is all free from the hand of the Father of grace. Jesus has paid the price for salvation of our spirit, soul, and body.

This is what gave Jesus the confidence to say, "Your sins are forgiven you," because He knew that everything for our spirit, soul, and body was covered in that promise. When we minister to unbelievers, we need to let them know that God will heal them because He wants them to be saved from every wicked work of the devil. Let them know that their sins and evils are forgiven as they receive Him.

> And when He had said this, He breathed on *them*, and said to them, "Receive the Holy Spirit. If you forgive the sins of any, they are forgiven them; if you retain the *sins* of any, they are retained."
>
> John 20:22-23, NKJV

Jesus released the Holy Spirit into the disciples. This was the day of salvation for them, when the Holy Spirit joined with their spirit man. When this happens to us, the Holy Spirit empowers us with authority as delegated influence. This allows us to release God's forgiveness of sin. Just as we have been studying in Jesus' life, we can retain sin as Paul did in Acts 13:11; commanding Elymas the sorcerer to go blind after he attempted to hinder the furtherance of the gospel. These acts can only be done under the leading and instruction of the Holy Spirit. Paul looked at Elymas and addressed him as the son of the devil and an enemy to righteousness. Forgiving sin is for all who will receive, but retained sins are for the evil in heart, the impenitent hearts. All we have to do is keep looking for people to help and bring them to the knowledge of God.

FAITH THAT HEALS

The power of the Lord must be present for the healing to happen. When the Holy Spirit is around, He always brings gifts for His children. The gifts of healings bring the power of restoration to heal all manner of illnesses. I believe that God increases the faith and the anointing based upon a person's faithfulness. This is true with any part of the faith walk. How much do the gifts of healings have to do with someone wanting to receive their healing? I believe that it has everything to do with it. If a person doesn't want to be healed, then it is virtually impossible. Now if a person wants to be healed and doesn't have faith, then, as I said before, I believe that God can override this lack of faith and do what I call a mercy healing. The unsaved receive mercy healings from the gifts of healings.

There are times where the gift is hindered by unbelief, bitterness, unwillingness to forgive, and many other reasons. Even though someone might have a desire to be completely healed, there are many reasons why the Holy Spirit wouldn't be able to heal them. This is one of the reasons we need the gifts of revelation to work with the other gifts.

After you have prayed for an individual and you know that the gift was active and they are not instantly healed, you may have to spend a few more minutes to build their faith. This can be done by teaching on faith, healing, love, or sharing a testimony of others who have been healed. Assure them that God desires to heal them. Send them home with scriptures to study. Many people feel very unworthy to receive; even though we all are unworthy and Jesus makes us worthy. Have them test the problem area several times, since they might not realize that God is at work in their body. Always ask them to do what they couldn't do before. When you have them do this, include that they shouldn't look for the symptoms; they should look for the healing. Finally, for the next twenty-four to forty-eight hours, have them thank the Lord for healing them. We have had many people healed by just taking a little extra time with instruction. We have sent people home sick with the instruction of just thanking God, and the next day, they returned to the meeting completely healed.

Thanksgiving is a great faith builder. God releases His power when their faith rises, and the healing virtue is released to them. I prayed for a little girl who had a lump on her shoulder. When she left, the lump was still there, but I told her to continue thanking Jesus for her healing. I saw her later and asked how long it took for the lump to disappear. She said it took three days, but she kept thanking God until it finally went away. That is faith as a mustard seed.

The enemy will always come to steal your healing, just like he lies about your salvation, speaking in tongues, and every blessing from above. Continue to thank God and write down when the healing took place. Yet, realize that the moment you prayed, the healing took place and needed faith through thanksgiving to reveal it.

> Then He said to the man, "Stretch out your hand." And he stretched *it* out, and it was restored as whole as the other.
>
> Matthew 12:13, NKJV

YOUR SINS ARE FORGIVEN YOU

A man with a withered hand came to Jesus with complete faith. When Jesus prayed for him, the man's hand was made whole through the gifts of healings. God released the virtue of healing into the man, and his hand was released and restored. Some accounts of healing are similar, but different in their display, and have the same results.

For example, the man came, and Jesus said, "Thy sins are forgiven."

Often the reason why people are encumbered or overcome with sickness or lack of health is because of sin. The gifts of healings are just that, they are gifts that release healing to forgive and cover sin. His blood cleansed us from sin. Although healing is associated with the stripes of Jesus, the whipping lashes on His back, forgiveness is released through the gifts of healings. Does that mean you can tell someone their sins are forgiven and they will go to Heaven? No, I am saying if someone is bound by guilt and their sickness has its roots in sin, but God wants to minister to them and heal them, you can say, "Your sins are forgiven, be healed." You have the right to forgive them of the repercussions of sin in their lives, but you do not have the right to reconcile them with God by forgiving their sins.

God gave me a revelation about something in a lady's past. She had anger against her father, and God said the reason the germs were released and began to generate inside her body and take control of her was because of anger. God gave revelation, and when I told her, she was cleansed in her heart and healed in her body. The gifts of healings are the power to cure all types of natural ailments, to forgive sins, and cause restoration in the physical, emotional, and spiritual realm. Holistic deliverance.

> And Jesus rebuked the demon, and it came out of him;
> and the child was cured from that very hour.
> Matthew 17:18, NKJV

Demons are cast out by one word through the gifts of healings. They are broken off by the gifts of healings. Jesus ordered the demon to leave the boy, and immediately the boy was cured.

Demons abiding in the flesh of a person cause sickness. Cancer is an evil spirit; many families suffer with this spirit for generations. The fact that Jesus overcame sickness is the reason why we can also cast out demons by the authority of God. Many sicknesses come from demonic activities and sin. Yes, wrong eating, hazardous elements, and pollution in the earth are also causes of many of the illnesses today. Nevertheless, these things are the repercussion of the fall of man, which is the very thing that Jesus died to deliver us from. Through the Word and the gifts of healings, the church will be free from sickness and demonic oppression and walk in divine health.

John G. Lake, said, "Healing was the evidence of God's forgiveness, heaven's testimony that their sins were remembered no more."

Heaven has sent a testimony that our sins have been forgiven. This testimony is healing, even the gifts of healings. Know that when the Lord calls you to operate in faith to heal all manner of sickness, He has called you to forgive their sins. This will result in their body, soul, or spirit being healed. As a note for practical application, the gifts of healings may also manifest with tangible feelings, such as heat or tingling on the palm of the hands, or as a confidence in the soul that the person or persons you pray for will positively be healed, without a shadow of a doubt.

CHAPTER 12

WORKING OF MIRACLES

To another the working of miracles.

1 Corinthians 12:10, NKJV

The working of miracles is the supernatural power to intervene into the ordinary course of nature and to counteract natural laws, if necessary. Both the gift of faith and the gift of healings can bring about a miracle.

John G. Lake classified the difference between miracles and healing in this way, "Healing is the restoration of what has already been, and a miracle is the creative power that brings about what has never been or is missing." Miracles supersede the natural, causing the natural to submit to the supernatural and allowing an effect (end result) to come about. There is no reasonable explanation for miracles. The Bible calls them infallible proofs; proof that cannot be refuted.

To whom He also presented Himself alive after His suffering by many infallible proofs, being seen by them
during forty days and speaking of the things pertaining
to the kingdom of God.

Acts 1:3, NKJV

WELL-ABLE WARRIORS

These infallible proofs (signs and wonders) are to show that Jesus is our
resurrected King and that He is the Lord of all. No one can refute a miracle worked by God. The devil, doctors, nor the self-righteous can deny
the powerful arm of the Lord.

In studying the workings of miracles, I learned that it is completely
dependent on us hearing Him, unlike the gifts of faith or healings in
which the Holy Spirit allows us to facilitate the application at certain
times. In this next passage, the Lord released the miracle working
power to Peter.

And Peter answered Him and said, "Lord, if it is You,
command me to come to You on the water." So He said,
"Come." And when Peter had come down out of the boat,
he walked on the water to go to Jesus.

Matthew 14:28-29, NKJV

WALKING ON WATER

When the Lord commanded Peter to step out of the boat, the miracle
working power was immediately available to hold Peter above the water.
The moment that Peter stepped out is when he received the end result
of this miracle working power. Peter walked on the water because he

believed the word that Jesus spoke, "Come." As soon as he heard the word, faith rose up in his heart. Because of this faith, God's miracle power caused him to walk above the laws of nature and enter into the supernatural realms of Jesus.

> His mother said to the servants, "Whatever He says to you, do *it*." Now there were set there six waterpots of stone, according to the manner of purification of the Jews, containing twenty or thirty gallons apiece. Jesus said to them, "Fill the waterpots with water." And they filled them up to the brim. And He said to them, "Draw *some* out now, and take it to the master of the feast." And they took *it*. When the master of the feast had tasted the water that was made wine, and did not know where it came from (but the servants who had drawn the water knew), the master of the feast called the bridegroom.
>
> John 2:5-9, NKJV

WATER INTO WINE

Again, we see that the miracle was manifested after simple obedience to the Word of the Lord. This is a supernatural occurrence; water has no way of becoming wine. Jesus worked an awesome miracle through the power of God. Workings of miracles actually mean the effect of dunamis power. The word "effect" is very important because it doesn't put an emphasis on the means to the miracle, it only concentrates on the end result of the dunamis power of God: the miracle.

The self-generating power of God (dunamis) causes miracles. The other operations are from an endowment (ability), where God enables us to facilitate His plan through dunamis power; the effect is the end result of dunamis power. God is going to decide how He desires to facilitate the miracle and we must obey Him. The other operations of power are classified as gifts, where miracles come from workings; working out the action in complete obedience to instruction. Gift means a gratuity or spiritual endowment; it is given to us to operate in authority. Gifts have been given to us for the purpose of using them as we are led by the Spirit. Workings are the end result of fulfilling a commanded blessing.

ADVENTURES OF OBEDIENCE

Philip was commanded to go to Gaza by the angel of the Lord. So, he prepared himself and went on this journey. The incredible thing about this part of the story is that Philip didn't even know why he was going, he just obeyed.

> Now an angel of the Lord spoke to Philip, saying, "Arise and go toward the south along the road which goes down from Jerusalem to Gaza." This is desert. So he arose and went.
>
> Acts 8:26-27, NKJV

He didn't gripe or complain, unlike many of us might. Even though it was a desert, he didn't refuse or rebut the instruction. The early disciples understood that if they could learn to trust the voice of the Lord, miracles would follow. When he reached Jerusalem, he ran into his assignment. Whenever the Lord tells you to go somewhere and He doesn't tell you why, then know for sure that you're like an angel on assignment. We rarely hear of these things today, simply because we don't walk in the same level of obedience as the early church. We will have these types of encounters as we learn to obey the governing voice of God. After Philip completed his assignment, a great working of miracles took place. The effect was to get him to the next assignment as soon as possible.

> So he commanded the chariot to stand still. And both Philip and the eunuch went down into the water, and he baptized him. Now when they came up out of the water, the Spirit of the Lord caught Philip away, so that the eunuch saw him no more; and he went on his way rejoicing. But Philip was found at Azotus. And passing through, he preached in all the cities till he came to Caesarea.
>
> Acts 8:38-40, NKJV

Philip was obedient to the voice of God to go to Gaza, and when he was finished with his work, the Lord changed the structure of his body and translated him to Azotus. At Azotus, there were people ordained to hear him preach the Word of the Lord. I do believe that the Lord can, at any given time, cause us to be used in the workings of miracles. If you study John G. Lake's life, you will notice that many times he would find himself translated to another town and ministering to someone the Lord had ordained him to touch. His lifestyle was one of submission and obedience. If you don't mind God interrupting your life with surprises, and you are willing to flow with Him in these bizarre circumstances, then I believe that you can look forward to some very exciting adventures in the near future. The days of workings of miracles are here and increasing every day. The key to an adventurous life in God is to obey Him at all costs.

PRACTICAL APPLICATION

Recognition: Recognize these gifts by the desires of your heart. The Lord allows us to have a desire for the things of God, and then He leads us and teaches us how to fulfill these desires. Some gifts will be easier to operate in because of your personality, motivational, and/or five-fold gifting. These power gifts will usually have a tangible expression accompanying them, such as tingling or heat in the hands and palms. This same heat could manifest in the same location in your body that is hurting in the person needing prayer. The working of miracles is much different in that it usually will give the persons involved an outward reward. Again, the working of miracles will bring faith to supersede the natural laws, bringing supernatural benefits. The keys to these operations are prayer and obedience. Obey the Lord, and His command will bring about miracles.

Operation: Power gifts are activated by stepping out in faith. Pray for everyone that you can, and you will find God's anointing when you expect it and when you don't expect it. After a while, the Holy Spirit will lead you with His unction. Be obedient to everything that God tells you to do, and the workings of miracles will become a part of your daily life.

Development: The Holy Spirit is the best teacher. As you step out in faith to touch people, He will be there to teach and lead you. During your personal devotions, ask the Holy Spirit to teach you in private about the different forms of anointing and gifts. In private, I learned to minister to hurting people before I even had an opportunity to minister. If you can't be foolish when you are all alone with just you and the Lord, you will never be able to overcome the fear of failure and insecurity that sometimes accompanies ministering in public.

In my private prayer times, I envisioned people walking out of wheelchairs. By the instruction of the Holy Spirit, I commanded demons to leave people's lives. One time, I was even used to bring a dead person back to life! The best way to learn anything is by role-playing; the same goes for the gifts of the Holy Spirit. Practice and role-play in private so that when the time arises that God needs you to go to work, you will know what to do.

CHAPTER 13

THE GIFTS OF UTTERANCE

**And they were all filled with the Holy Spirit
and began to speak with other tongues,
as the Spirit gave them utterance.**

Acts 2:4, NKJV

Shortly after I devoted my life to Christ, also referred to as being saved or born again, for anyone new to Christianity, I was at a Phil Driscoll concert. Phil is a singer-musician who plays the trumpet and other wind instruments. Sitting amongst a crowd of twenty-five hundred people, the prophetic anointing came upon me. I stood up and started speaking loudly in tongues as Phil Driscoll was talking between songs. Usually, this experience would be followed by interpretation of tongues, which would let those in the room know God's intention. I personally had never given an interpretation of tongues before. Every time I was used to give a message in tongues, someone else would give the interpretation. I had also never released a direct prophetic word at that time. I was a one-hit wonder, and I was singing that song everywhere. This was a real step in faith to speak out in tongues in front of twenty-five hundred people. After I gave the message in tongues, I quickly sat down and waited for someone to interpret. All I knew was that I felt the power of God all over me to speak. I didn't understand the difference between a corporate prophetic word and a tongue and interpretation. The effect is the same, but the administration of them is different. So, there I was with hundreds of people looking my way, waiting for the interpretation.

Just as I started to become nervous, Phil Driscoll gave the interpretation and followed the word of the Lord with an altar call. It was a powerful moment of obedience for me. The Lord is not interested in our dignity. He was testing me to see if I would obey Him no matter what the circumstances. Do not be ashamed to look stupid when you know that God is moving you, He will always cover your back as long as you are stepping out by His unction. Even if you make a mistake, God will cover your shame. He is a loving God.

The first time God asked me to stand up and speak in tongues like that, I didn't realize what was happening to me. I was in a service led by the pastor who had been so gracious to work with me in my first years as a Christian. He helped me develop character and trained me in the proper use of the spiritual gifts. The experience was unforgettable. My heart started pounding and I didn't know if I was under fear (an anxiety attack) or some ungodly control; it was very intense and tangible. I began praying for God to take this feeling from me. Immediately, it left. At that moment, I realized that it was not from the devil, but that it was God moving on me, but for what reason? I asked the Holy Spirit to explain what was occurring, and He brought clarity to me and explained that it was the gift of tongues. All He desired from me was to speak out in tongues. The Holy Spirit has always been my teacher and, believe me, He is the best teacher there is. I vowed that if He would give me another chance, I would obey. My greatest fear was to disappoint God, so I purposed in my mind that I would do anything that He asked of me. I was more afraid of displeasing God than I was of displeasing man.

The following week, I was nervous about stepping into this new realm of God. Similar to the previous week, my heart started pounding and I broke out in a sweat. It felt as if I was having an anxiety attack. I wanted to get this over with, so I stood up and I started yelling in tongues, right in the middle of the pastor's message. It is never God's intention to interrupt the service and/or the message, so be very sensitive to the time and circumstances that you are in before you step out. You may just interrupt God speaking through someone else if you don't maintain control. Ask me how I know! During this brief moment of ecstasy, I felt as if my spirit man was pulled out of my body and thrown back into my body three or four times. I had worked myself into such a state of emotion that I was totally drained!

My hope in sharing these embarrassing stories is that you will, first of all, lose all fear of making a mistake and, secondly, avoid some pitfalls. Please don't follow my example of ignorance but follow the example of never giving up. When all of the yelling was done, I sat back down. I didn't notice the reaction of the pastor nor anyone else because my eyes were closed, and I had no intention of looking around. There was the longest silence that I had ever experienced. Then, finally, someone stood and uttered the message. I was so relieved! Later, my pastor pulled me to the side and said, "I like it that you are stepping out in this way, but there is a proper time to release the word. When I am speaking is not the time. Wait until there is a gap in the service." I encourage you the same way. Wait until there is an opening that will not disturb the flow of the Spirit or the order of the meeting.

The gift of prophecy, diverse kinds of tongues, and interpretation of tongues are recognized as the gifts of utterance. Their purpose is to declare, proclaim, and establish God's will and intentions through verbal communication. It is God speaking and instructing man by using another human being. These gifts do not only operate for revelation's sake; their sole purpose is to declare the given revelation with power.

CHAPTER 14

PROPHECY

...to another prophecy...

1 Corinthians 12:10, NKJV

Prophecy is a supernatural utterance in the native tongue; it is a miracle of divine utterance not conceived by human reason or thought. It includes speaking unto men for edification, exhortation, comfort, and future events.

The exciting thing about the gift of prophecy is that it works with so many other gifts. Because of this uniqueness, it creates faith that results in a miracle. If you study the prophetic ministry of the Old and New Testaments, you see that each time the Word of the Lord was spoken, it created an atmosphere for God to move. The result was either a miracle or judgment. The word of God creates change in people, atmospheres, mindsets, and life in general. The gift of prophecy works miracles. First of all, everything that you prophesy must first be revealed to your spirit and soul. It's a miracle of divine information and expectation. Prophecy is a promise of God's action, power, and intervention.

Whatever the power that follows, there should always be a release of power to bring about the promise. If God is not telling you to speak the promise, please do not speak; you'll only cause more harm than help. Instead, it's much better to focus in prayer on that revelation.

Remember that there is an anointing that accompanies each one of these gifts. The Holy Spirit will teach you about the different gifts and enable you to recognize which anointing goes with each gift. The only access to the gifts of the Holy Spirit is through His anointing. Jesus, Himself, was anointed. The only question is, how do you know that you are anointed? You should always be able to recognize when the anointing is upon you for work. When the anointing comes upon you to prophesy, the Lord will speak to you by giving you a word, inspiration, or a vision. In the beginning, you may only receive one word or a simple impression. Faithfully use these "first level visions" and God will increase them. For example, you see a stream, it is moving down the road, then it is coming into the person's house, flowing all over their family. Although this may not make any sense to you, don't hesitate to share these dark sayings. The person receiving will understand completely what God is trying to get across. These prophetic visions or words are known as dark sayings or proverbs: word pictures that give a message. It may be dark or not understandable to anyone except the hearer. You are following a picture. For some, it will be like a movie, and as you see the vision, you describe the vision. These forms of the prophetic can be very encouraging to you as well as the hearer when released in the heart and intent of God. Prophecy brings a certain emotion or zeal in response to the revelation.

As the deliverer of a prophetic word, you should feel the heart of God as you speak. Otherwise, it is a misrepresentation of what God is saying.

Sometimes, when you hear the voice of God, it can be one word that He gives you. This shouldn't concern you because once you start to deliver the word, God will give you the rest. I have experienced this many times. For example, I will hear the word "increase," and when I approach the person to deliver the word, the Lord gives me the rest of the prophecy. I would say something like, "I hear the word increase," followed by, "you have been experiencing challenges that are decreasing you, but God says that you will begin to experience increase." I should be clear that, if the person is an unbeliever and is unfamiliar with prophecy, I would be less direct and more inquisitive. Similar to Jesus with the woman at the well. Once there is an obvious openness, I would share the prophetic word. It could go like this, still working with the word "increase." "Hi, my name is Tracey. What do you do for work? The economy is going through a bit of a change, would you agree? May I encourage you with something? I often get pretty strong impressions around people, and this may sound strange, but I get the impression that increase or a promotion may be around the corner for you." This will often open up the conversation even more. Trust the Lord for more detailed revelation. The more specific the words are, the more it will help the receiver to believe that it was specifically for them. I am not saying that simple words are ineffective because any word from the Lord is effective. There's just nothing like the feeling you get when the Lord has pinpointed you and declares a great desire for your life.

> And even things without life giving sound, whether pipe
> or harp, except they give a distinction in the sounds,

how shall it be known what is piped or harped? For if the trumpet give an uncertain sound, who shall prepare himself to the battle? So likewise ye, except ye utter by the tongue words easy to be understood, how shall it be known what is spoken? for ye shall speak into the air. There are, it may be, so many kinds of voices in the world, and none of them is without signification.

1 Corinthians 14:7-10, KJV

Encouragement comes when we give a distinct sound that can be understood. This is reason enough to seek the Lord for more distinction when trying to encourage someone.

The gifts of revelation work with the gift of prophecy. As soon as they are given for the purpose of speech and/or communication, it becomes a gift of utterance. The misunderstanding is that prophetic revelation isn't given before it is delivered. But as I covered in earlier chapters, it would be spiritually illegal for God to take control of your conscience and will. Your mind must receive the revelation before you utter it. The key is to receive the revelation and speak it without trying to subject it to your human logic and reasoning.

The prophetic gift is increased by the reason of use. If you want the gift to increase, use the gift! After a while, you may be given people's names and addresses to confirm the Word of the Lord. This brings us to the next point: at the beginning of operating in the gift of prophecy, you might not have a confirmation to follow your gift. But as you become comfortable with your gift, you should ask the Lord for some type of confirmation to build the faith of the people. Moses had a confirmation. Samuel confirmed what would take place in Saul's life before he was crowned king.

And Judas and Silas, being prophets also themselves, exhorted the brethren with many words, and
confirmed them.

Acts 15:32, KJV

In this passage, the word "confirmed" means to reestablish. God
used something to reestablish the words that He had already spoken. It
could be distinct words like addresses and names, or it could be the gift
of healing or the gift of faith. There is no limitation. God wants to make
Himself plain and clear.

Always speak as you would normally speak. God wants to use you,
not a religious version of you. Speak in your native tongue; if King James
English is not your native tongue, then don't prophecy in the King's
English. If you speak Ebonics (so called street lingo), then you should
prophesy accordingly. Speak the way you are accustomed to speaking.
Go back to the original text of the Bible or be normal. Say what God is
saying as clearly as you can but stay away from adding things to it. No
matter how many times you trip over your words, if you receive the miracle working power behind it, you will see the evidence.

The other thing that you don't necessarily need to add is, "Thus says
God." People will know if you're speaking in the Name of the Lord or
not. Many people put so much emphasis on saying this that it can be a
distraction. If you are afraid to even call it a Word of the Lord because it
is new or you may not be sure, don't be pressured to label it as such. Just
say, "I feel." Just be free and allow God to use you. But by no means be
reckless with the Word of the Lord. Just be free.

The gift of prophecy includes speaking unto men for edification,
exhortation, and comfort. That is very important. The prophetic ministry of the New Testament is different, in many ways, from the Old

Testament prophetic ministry. I believe that most Christians will never be called upon by the Lord to rebuke someone prophetically. If judgment is to come through the prophetic, it should come through the prophetic office, not the gift of prophecy used by someone who is not called to the five-fold ministry. God is always interested in His goodness drawing someone to repentance before He chooses to release His judgment. If God must judge, it will be His last resort. The New Testament prophetic voice must be filtered through the grace of God.

Yes, sometimes you will see that God does judge, but it is done in the character and nature of God, love and grace! Judgment doesn't come before God has tried to edify them, encourage them, and exhort them out of a lifestyle of sin and disobedience. We see God's judgment in action in the story of Ananias and Sapphira. That was real judgment in the body of Christ. It is going to come back to the church. We should not be afraid of this type of judgment returning to the church unless we plan on lying to the Holy Spirit. It is New Testament! The majority of the ministry that you are given in the prophetic word will fall under the categories of edification, exhortation, and comfort.

Exhortation is instruction, edification is lifting someone up, and comforting is consoling someone. If they need love and care, then you give it to them. Whatever it takes to edify them to a better place. If God ever gives you a word of warning for someone, He never puts him or her in a place of condemnation. He always gives them a way up and out.

Let me give you an example of a godly rebuke that gives a way out. "Ma'am, you have been living in adultery. God says, get out, or you will find yourself in a terrible physical condition because I see the enemy coming, and he is going to try to destroy your body. You must give up this relationship and come out of adultery. If you get out of adultery, God will take you to another level where you no longer will have the guilt or the shame. It all will be removed, and God's plan will be established for your life." There is never condemnation. There is only edification. All you are doing is warning them of the repercussions of their actions. But, when you hear from God, there will be a way out. The Holy Spirit never condemns, He always convicts and gives people a way out of their state of reproach. When you minister the Word of the Lord, it should comfort them. Sometimes people just need to know that Jesus loves them. Sometimes people just need to know that God wants to wrap His arms around them.

Half of the job of giving a prophetic word is to remove anything that would keep the receiver from trusting the word of the Lord because of the package that the word comes in. Always seek to build trust. Don't charge in, thinking that you're God's man or woman who's going to save the day. It doesn't help at all! The humble route is always the best route.

Why would God desire to use you to prophesy to someone? Prophecy gives direction when there is none, gives hope when hope is gone, peace where there is no peace, and destiny to a destitute life. After Peter denied Jesus, he went back to fishing. When Jesus found Peter, Peter had been fishing all night long. Laboring in vain! Jesus then led Peter through a series of questions. I call this "courting him back." When Peter was in a place to hear, the Lord began to prophesy to him. Let's read it together.

> "Most assuredly, I say to you, when you were younger, you girded yourself and walked where you wished; but when you are old, you will stretch out your hands, and another will gird you and carry *you* where you do not wish." This He spoke, signifying by what death he would glorify God. And when He had spoken this, He said to him, "Follow Me."
>
> John 21:18-19, NKJV

A CONDITION TO THE PROMISE

The Lord revealed the future to Peter. I am sure that, at the time, this word didn't make any sense to Peter, but later it would prove itself to be accurate and a tool of strength in his life. Every prophetic word has conditions on it. The Lord added the final words, "FOLLOW ME." Many people would have ignored this command. Yes, it is a command, not a suggestion. It is a condition to the word of the Lord coming true. For example, many times, the Lord will encourage someone with a word concerning their finances, stating that He desires to bless them. Let's be very realistic. Yes, God wants to bless, but if you're not in covenant with Him, how can He bless you? If you don't pay tithes, how can He bypass His written Word of covenant and bless you? The Word says that you rob God and as a result, you will become the recipient of a curse.

I have said to churches prophetically that if they would continue what they were doing, the Lord would bring a great increase. The funny thing is, most of the people only heard that the Lord was going to bring great increase, and they stopped doing what the Lord had asked of them. So, the increase stopped. The prophetic should remove all second-guessing of whether or not it is going to come to pass, but often it causes more second-guessing when people try to process it with their natural understanding. The Word of the Lord usually challenges all reason.

Later in Peter's life, we see the reason why God spoke the Word. When you receive or give a word, you must understand that it is given for a reason and often with conditions. Either they are in a time that they need to use it for war, or they will soon need it for war.

> This charge I commit to you, son Timothy, according to
> the prophecies previously made concerning you, that by
> them you may wage the good warfare, having faith and

a good conscience, which some having rejected, concerning the faith have suffered shipwreck.

1 Timothy 1:18-19, NKJV

God gives the prophetic to give us power to wage a good warfare in
keeping faith and a good conscience. These are the two things that the
devil is trying to take from us. If the devil can take these things, then
he can cause us to be shipwrecked and abort our destiny while casting
away purpose.

The Lord was equipping Peter to fight a good fight in the future.
When you speak to people in the Name of the Lord, you are equipping
them to fight a good fight. Sometimes it is hard for you or the person
that you give the word to, to understand why you are giving the word.
Never allow current understanding to prevent you from engaging the
word with faith.

> And as we stayed many days, a certain prophet named
> Agabus came down from Judea. When he had come to
> us, he took Paul's belt, bound his *own* hands and feet,
> and said, "Thus says the Holy Spirit, 'So shall the Jews at
> Jerusalem bind the man who owns this belt, and deliver
> *him* into the hands of the Gentiles.'" Now when we heard
> these things, both we and those from that place pleaded
> with him not to go up to Jerusalem. Then Paul answered,
> "What do you mean by weeping and breaking my heart?
> For I am ready not only to be bound, but also to die at
> Jerusalem for the name of the Lord Jesus." So when he
> would not be persuaded, we ceased, saying, "The will of
> the Lord be done."

Acts 21:10-14, NKJV

Agabus delivered the word of the Lord to Paul regarding the trials that he would come under if he were to go to Jerusalem. I'm sure that Agabus thought that this word would discourage Paul from going, because it described some tough times ahead. Of course, if you gave a word like this today, you would be kicked out of many churches and called a heretic. The truth of the matter is, that if he had given any word other than the truth, it would have been in conflict with what God was planning for Paul. Believe it or not, it was the will of God for Paul to go through these trials, and that's why the Lord prophesied to him—to encourage him to continue because God was with him. Remember that the Holy Spirit is in charge of the gifts, and He will deliver the right word as long as we keep our agenda out of the way. When the rest of the company who were with Paul and Agabus heard this word, they immediately tried to convince Paul not to go. A prophetic word is for those times when people around you don't agree with the word of the Lord and you can, with confidence, defy all human reasoning and demonic wavering.

PUBLIC PROPHECY

I once went to a church where the pastor asked me not to speak the prophetic words into the microphone; he preferred for me to whisper it into the people's ears. The reason being that in the past, people were harassed by some in his congregation about the time that it was taking for it to come to pass. The truth of the matter is that, in due season, all will see the profiting of the word in God's timing, not ours.

There are many reasons why a prophetic minister shouldn't whisper the word into people's ears unless the Holy Spirit leads you to do it that way (usually, if it is a rebuke that others need not hear or very private information that others should not hear). First, how can the other prophetic ministers test the word, as instructed in 1 Corinthians 14? How can the word be accurately recorded and documented for the times when the person really needs to hear it again? It is scriptural to record the prophetic words; otherwise, we would not have many parts of the Old and New Testament. Lastly, if you can't handle people bugging you about the promise, how are you going to overcome the devil when he comes and tells you that it will never come to pass? How can you be strong, holding on to the word that says, "You shall live and not die," when the doctor comes and says that you have the HIV virus? We have to learn to be tough. If we can be moved by a few people who don't understand what God is saying, then how can we fight when all odds are against us? Agabus was only confirming what the Holy Spirit had been saying in every city that Paul would enter. Read it here.

> And see, now I go bound in the spirit to Jerusalem, not knowing the things that will happen to me there, except that the Holy Spirit testifies in every city, saying that chains and tribulations await me. But none of these things move me; nor do I count my life dear to myself, so that I may finish my race with joy, and the ministry which I received from the Lord Jesus, to testify to the gospel of the grace of God.
>
> Acts 20:22-24, NKJV

The word of the Lord bound Paul in his spirit and strengthened Paul so that nothing could move him from the purpose of God. We can handle the storms of life if we know that God is walking through the storms with us. We know that God cares enough to warn us of the next season of growth to prepare us for the following season of promotion. Whether uplifting or warning, when the word of the Lord comes, it should put a faith and good conscience in us. Then we can say the same thing that Paul said, "None of these things move me, I don't count my life dear to myself, but I am willing to do anything to accomplish the mission of the Lord for my life." This confidence is what allowed Peter to fall asleep when he was in jail and Herod threatened his life.

> And when Herod was about to bring him out, that night Peter was sleeping, bound with two chains between two soldiers; and the guards before the door were keeping the prison. Now behold, an angel of the Lord stood by *him*, and a light shone in the prison; and he struck Peter on the side and raised him up, saying, "Arise quickly!" And his chains fell off *his* hands. Then the angel said to him, "Gird yourself and tie on your sandals"; and so he did. And he said to him, "Put on your garment and follow me." So he went out and followed him, and did not know that what was done by the angel was real, but thought he was seeing a vision.
>
> Acts 12:6-9, NKJV

Right before our eyes is the fulfillment of Peter's prophecy. Before this time, it didn't make much sense, but now it is perfectly clear. Peter was so confident that this couldn't be his day to die because the Lord had already told him how he would die. It wasn't that Peter didn't believe that Herod could kill him, I am sure that the event of James' beheading was enough to confirm to Peter that Herod was psychotically lunatic enough to kill him. Also, with two bad smelling guards sleeping next to Peter, it was enough to give him the reality of the situation. With all these things proving that it was going to be the end of his life in less than twenty-four hours, Peter could still fall asleep. I am sure that Peter rehearsed in his mind how the Lord would free him, like most of us when we trust the Lord to deliver us. The Lord is much more creative than we are.

Going back to the word of the Lord, Jesus proclaimed that when Peter was young, he would gird himself. We see the first manifestation of the prophetic promise in this passage of scripture when the angel said to him, "Gird yourself and tie on your sandals." At this point, we know that Peter was not to die that morning. Although, there is no clue to Peter's age, we can assume that he was still young because they didn't carry him where he didn't want to go. God gives us prophetic words so that we can sleep in the midst of the storm like Jesus did in the boat and Peter in the jail.

Without getting too deep, I would like to give brief instruction and understanding to the gift of prophecy. First of all, the gift of prophecy has two focal points. The first is corporate (where God will speak through individuals to a body or group of people). The second is individual prophecies (God using an individual to speak to another individual). Going back to the example of me giving an utterance in tongues for the first time and not having the interpretation, I felt hot all over my body, my heart started beating rapidly, and my hands became sweaty when the unction of the Lord fell on me to prophesy. This has happened to many of you as you were sitting in church or a Bible study and you didn't have any idea what to do or what was going on. Before I continue, I must clarify something: once the gift of tongues is interpreted, the end result is like a prophetic word. As soon as the tongue or heavenly language is interpreted, it is transformed into edification.

> I wish you all spoke with tongues, but even more that
> you prophesied; for he who prophesies *is* greater than
> he who speaks with tongues, unless indeed he interprets,

that the church may receive edification.

1 Corinthians 14:5, NKJV

I will cover more about the gift of tongues later. The one thing that I wanted to make clear is that there is a tongue and interpretation that falls under the category of the gift of prophecy. The Bible clearly states that prophecy is for edification of the church. In the context of this scripture, Paul is only referring to the church at this point, not to individual prophetic words. If we will remember that the epistles were written to address certain problems in the apostolic churches, then we will have a better understanding of what was written. Without going into the details of the problem, we must understand that Paul was addressing the use of the corporate gift of prophecy and the corporate gift of tongues and interpretation in the early part of 1 Corinthians chapter 14.

Many people will start out using their corporate prophetic gift by sounding the trumpet of tongues beforehand, because they are new to the gift of prophecy. They are speaking the same message in two different languages: heavenly and earthly. This is the way the Holy Spirit introduced me to prophecy. I first started off by speaking in tongues and allowing an interpreter to interpret. Then, as I gained confidence, realizing that God wanted to use me, the Lord started giving me the interpretation.

Again, in verse 5, Paul writes, "Unless indeed he interprets," describing the person giving the tongue. From this point, I gained confidence and the Lord bypassed the trumpet and gave the direct prophecy. There are times when I will still give the tongue and interpretation or someone else will give the interpretation. So, it is not something that is less important, yet for a novice, it is a wonderful way the Holy Spirit teaches us to prophesy. It takes the pressure off the rookie and allows someone of more experience to take control.

If you feel like God is trying to get your attention in a service, this is a great way to gain confidence for operating in a corporate prophetic anointing. Remember, always find out what the protocol of your church is for corporate prophetic words. It will always be more beneficial to you, your pastor, and your church if you submit yourself to the guidance of the leadership. Sometimes it will feel as if you cannot control yourself, but this is not so. You have control of the gift as far as the timing of releasing the word is concerned.

> And the spirits of the prophets are subject to the prophets.
>
> 1 Corinthians 14:32, NKJV

I have said, myself, and have heard others use this excuse often, "I just couldn't help myself." Or even, "Who are you to stop the word of the Lord?" In the past, I've said this many times and later realized that it was just my arrogance speaking.

Another way to release a word for the first time is to write it on a piece of paper and deliver it to the pastor or a leader of the church. I remember when I drove down to California from Washington state, I heard that there was a small church in northern California having a church service, so I stopped by. As soon as I walked in, the Lord gave me a word for that church. So instead of standing up and spouting off, I wrote down the word and gave it to an usher. The usher was so excited that he quickly passed it to the pastor, who immediately stood up and read it. This was exciting. Even though the congregation didn't know who had received and delivered the word, it was exciting to know that they were blessed. Never go into a new church and start prophesying.

Individual words are just as exciting. At first, when the Lord is trying to get your attention, you will feel, to some extent, the same things that you feel when you get a corporate word. That is if you feel anything. I have covered how to approach people in earlier chapters. The main things are to make sure that you get their permission to speak to them. If not, don't cast pearls before swine. That's the phrase the Bible uses for wasting your time on someone who won't listen and receive what you have to say. And don't always expect people to understand everything you say at the time you say it. Many times, I will speak to someone about a situation in their life or family, and they will have no knowledge of it until they go home and get the news. Often, people are so shocked at the fact that God is speaking to them that they can't remember anything. They come up to us later and tell us that they remembered who or what we were talking about. Never try to interpret for someone what God is saying to them unless the Lord has, for sure, shown you what He means. It will cause trouble for you as well as the person listening to your advice.

Sometimes, while you are prophesying, you may think to yourself, "What am I saying?" Don't be alarmed, nine out of ten times it is the Lord speaking through you. I remember praying for a young guy about twelve or thirteen years old who had a major back problem. While I was praying for him, the Lord showed me that the boy would be healed within fourteen days, so I spoke this over him and prayed a prayer of agreement. A year later, while sitting in a Benny Hinn crusade, this young man's mother came over to me and told me about the miracle that took place in her son's back within the time period that was spoken. But I remember how I felt after the anointing lifted. I was sitting at home rehearsing the different prophetic words and miracles in my head. I thought to myself, "What did I say? Fourteen days?" After the anointing lifts and you're at home thinking on the course of the day, don't let the devil get you thinking that you missed it before God has a chance to bring it to pass. The worst thing is when a person says that they speak in the Name of the Lord under His unction and then, when the anointing lifts, they change their mind before God can even confirm anything. If you take it back, you tie the hands of God. That is, the word is conditional to specific action. I once gave a word to a man about a property that he was looking to purchase. I had no knowledge of the property beforehand. I told him that a problem would arise with the property but that he should continue the purchase, for God would work a miracle. He confirmed that they were in contract for that property. A little time passed, and they found an issue with the property. He decided to pull out of the contract and missed the miracle. Later, his pastor wanted me to apologize for missing it. I was willing to admit that I had inaccurately prophesied until I heard that they didn't follow the condition of the word. People believe that the prophetic must make sense in order to believe. I only have one question: why are the Jews still believing and praying every day for the Gaza strip, rebuilding of the temple, and the return of the Messiah? They know that prophecy fulfilled needs some men to participate and to be courageous enough to believe for the unbelievable. Most of the time, when you feel like this word is too wild for God, watch out, it just may be God.

Another incident happened while I was in Wisconsin in a church service. The Lord showed me a young man who had cancer. God spoke a word to the boy, saying this cancer would leave as fast as it came, within six months. Every time his parents would take him to treatment, they would say, "Thank You, Lord that we only have four more months of this to endure." Then three months, then two months. How could cancer fight this type of faith in God's prophetic words? Most of us take the prophetic word so lightly. Today, this young man is completely healed by the prophetic word; an utterance of miracle-working power. Step out of the boat and allow God to use you to edify the Body of Christ.

CHAPTER 15

DIVERSE KINDS OF TONGUES

...to another [different] kinds of tongues...

1 Corinthians 12:10, NKJV

There are three different uses of the gift of tongues: prophecy, prayer, and the communication of the gospel. Both prophecy and the communication of the gospel are God speaking to man His eternal plan. The prayer language is the Holy Spirit making intercession for us and through us, speaking mysteries to God (see 1 Corinthians 14:2).

> Likewise the Spirit also helps in our weaknesses. For we
> do not know what we should pray for as we ought, but

the Spirit Himself makes intercession for us with groan-
ings which cannot be uttered.

Romans 8:26, NKJV

The purpose of praying in the heavenly language is to have the ability
to intercede and pray with power. Praying in the Spirit is also a key to
hearing the voice of God and living in His power. We all should have this
gift of praying in the heavenly language. Again, this is not a deep dive
into this gift but an overview to help you start a more in-depth study of
the subject. I would like to give scriptural references for the need and
availability of this prayer language.

> Then Peter said to them, "Repent, and let every one
> of you be baptized in the name of Jesus Christ for the
> remission of sins; and you shall receive the gift of the
> Holy Spirit. For the promise is to you and to your chil-
> dren, and to all who are afar off, as many as the Lord
> our God will call."
>
> Acts 2:38-39, NKJV

This scripture alone is enough to confirm that God wants every
believer to receive the gift of the Holy Spirit. The only people who cannot
receive this gift are the ones whom Jesus never called, and we know by
the scriptures that Jesus called everyone. All are called! So, this promise is for you! It doesn't matter what denomination you belong to. That
means Catholic, Lutheran, Presbyterian, Baptist, Pentecostal, Charis-
matic or any other denomination not mentioned here. All who confess
Jesus must be filled and gifted by the Holy Spirit. Jesus said that we will
be filled with the Holy Spirit and then His power will fill us. The promise

is that we would receive power after the Holy Spirit has come upon us (see Acts 1:8). When the unction of the Holy Spirit came upon the disciples, there came an utterance from them and they spoke with other tongues. Let's look at this scripture.

> Now when the Day of Pentecost had fully come, they were all with one accord in one place. And suddenly there came a sound from heaven, as of a rushing mighty wind, and it filled the whole house where they were sitting. Then there appeared to them divided tongues, as of fire, and *one* sat upon each of them. And they were all filled with the Holy Spirit and began to speak with other tongues, as the Spirit gave them utterance.
>
> Acts 2:1-4, NKJV

On the Day of Pentecost, the Holy Spirit first filled the room and then filled the people in the room. The word "filled" means that He crammed Himself into the room and then crammed Himself into the people. Why would God cram Himself into a room? It's simple; to change the atmosphere. Why, then, did He cram Himself into the people? Again, to change the people. When He crammed Himself into the room, it changed the atmosphere and made it a place where He could change the people. He filled the people to give them a new language. The Holy Spirit gave them the utterance. The key to the gift of tongues is that the Holy Spirit gives the utterance.

When I first received Jesus as my savior, I was filled with the Holy Spirit and spoke in other tongues. The people praying for me were praying in other tongues over me. As they were praying, I was thinking, "How do I do this, what language will I speak, maybe I'll speak Arabic." On top of these things going through my head, I was slightly intoxicated with four 16 oz. bottles of imported beer. At the time, I was accustomed to having at least two beers with my dinner. So, I went to this meeting after having dinner, and I was a little buzzed. But after a few minutes of prayer, I stopped listening to them and heard a still small voice (utterance) in my heart, and I repeated what the Holy Spirit was telling me to say.

I hope that this blows away every religious thought that any of you have had about being perfect before you can be filled. Jesus fills you to help you become perfect. When Peter preached to the Gentiles in Cornelius' home, they were filled and spoke with tongues and magnified God. In Ephesus, Paul and John laid hands on the disciples and they were filled with the Holy Spirit, spoke in other tongues, and prophesied.

After Peter and the disciples left the upper room, men from every nation under the sun were in Jerusalem and heard them speaking in their native tongues. This was an incredible miracle. God reversed the curse that was once sent upon man when man thought that they were self-sufficient enough to build a tower to reach God. God spoke from Heaven and confused the tongues of men. At Jesus' death, God brought complete restoration to us by giving us gifts that would return us back to our original state of communion with God. Better yet, rather than just being God's creation, He made us His sons and daughters. The Holy Spirit brought us into restoration by changing their tongues so that all could understand what God was saying. I believe that in these last days we will find this gift more active in the delivery and reception of the gospel.

> And when this sound occurred, the multitude came
> together, and were confused, because everyone heard

them speak in his own language. Then they were all amazed and marveled, saying to one another, "Look, are not all these who speak Galileans? And how *is it that* we hear, each in our own language in which we were born? Parthians and Medes and Elamites, those dwelling in Mesopotamia, Judea and Cappadocia, Pontus and Asia, Phrygia and Pamphylia, Egypt and the parts of Libya adjoining Cyrene, visitors from Rome, both Jews and proselytes, Cretans and Arabs—we hear them speaking in our own tongues the wonderful works of God."

Acts 2:6-11, NKJV

The purpose of this particular use of the gift of tongues is to communicate the gospel to those whom you could not speak to in your natural ability. Many misled people think that this gift is received by natural learning. If this was true, how could it be a gift (endowment) of the Holy Spirit? I know of an elderly woman who had this gift operating in her life. She was taking a cab in a foreign country. She didn't speak the language and she gave the driver instructions on a note. The driver took off and started driving in the wrong direction. As she noticed that he was going the wrong way, she began praying in other tongues and, without her knowledge, the Holy Spirit began to speak through her to the man in his native language. The man stopped the car and turned around to look at this lady and said in English, "How can you speak my language?" The man fully understood English the whole time, but pretended as if he didn't understand her until the Lord rebuked him. As she explained that she didn't know his language, but her God did, the man began to cry and tell her what the Lord had said through her. The Holy Spirit rebuked the man for his evil heart and demanded that he repent and give his life to Jesus. The man was so fearful that he made her leave his cab. This woman was saved through the gift of tongues. As the church truly begins to understand this gift and expect God to move in this way, the nations of the world will open up to the gospel in a way like never before. Nations can be turned in a day by such a powerful manifestation as the gift of tongues.

CHAPTER 16

INTERPRETATION OF TONGUES

...to another the interpretation of tongues.

1 Corinthians 12:10, NKJV

A few times, while overseas, I experienced the gift of interpretation of a native tongue. I didn't hear it in my ears, but I understood it in my heart. It was more of a knowing. It wasn't for a long period of time. I believe for the ability to operate in both the gift of interpretation of the native tongue as well as the ability to speak in other foreign languages by the Spirit of God. On the day of Pentecost, men heard the message of God by the Holy Spirit. The Holy Spirit initiated this, but when it comes to tongues in prayer and prophecy, we can ask for the interpretation.

> Wherefore let him that speaketh in an unknown tongue
> pray that he may interpret. For if I pray in an unknown
> tongue, my spirit prayeth, but my understanding
> is unfruitful.
>
> 1 Corinthians 14:13-14, KJV

Again, this scripture confirms that there is a gift that enables us to pray to God, and unless we have the interpretation, we will not have understanding. For most of us, it is good for our spirits to pray without our minds having understanding so that fear, doubt, and other hindrances that the human mind produces cannot keep God from being magnified in our lives. Paul's thought towards this was, why not have both the ability to pray with understanding and without understanding?

Praying without understanding doesn't mean praying in tongues and reading a magazine. It means to pray in tongues and think on Jesus, unless the Lord is giving understanding through the gift of interpretation. I remember a time when I was ministering to a young man in my youth ministry, and we were praying in tongues. As he was praying, I began to see flashes of his family, and his brother, in particular, was standing out to me. After he finished praying, I told him what he was praying for. He said that his brother was indeed heavy on his heart. This was the interpretation of his tongue or prayer language. Sometimes, when I am praying, I will get the understanding of what the Spirit is praying by visions, impressions, or a still small voice of the Holy Spirit. Sometimes it is so subtle that I could confuse it with my own conscience. Next time you pray in the Spirit, pray that the Lord will give you the interpretation of what you are praying for, and then look for subtle intuitions or nudges of the Holy Spirit. After a time of seeking for this, you will begin to recognize how the gift works.

In some of our meetings, the Lord will lead me to have the person that I am ministering to pray in the Spirit. Then the Holy Spirit gives me the interpretation of their prayer and the answer to their prayer.

Interpretation of the gift of tongues that is spoken corporately is very similar to how the prophetic gift operates. But it can only be initiated by the release of the gift of tongues. A person can't give an interpretation unless there is something to be interpreted. I have heard many people say that it is an interpretation versus a translation, but they are straining at gnats by using the English definition of this word. The actual word is *hermeneia* (her-may-ni-ah), in the Greek, which means translation. Although this is the meaning of the word, the idea is that it is a translation of purpose and definition, not one of words.

When the utterance in tongues is released, the interpreter will start to feel the unction. As I stated earlier, the manifestation of the anointing may not be the same. You may not even experience any tangible feeling, but God must get your attention somehow to let you know that it is you who must give the interpretation. Just open your mouth and let the revelation go. With the interpretation of tongues and prophecy, you will not receive all of the word at the time of utterance. The Lord will deliver the revelation as you start, so you must always be willing to take a step in faith. Don't worry, God will never let you down.

While you're being used in these gifts, never be ashamed of any mistakes that you might make. This is all part of stepping out. If people give you a hard time and they aren't willing to teach you how to do it properly, most of the time they have never been used of God through that gift.

THE UTTERANCE GIFTS:
PRACTICAL APPLICATION

RECOGNITION:

Recognize these gifts by the desires of your heart. The Lord allows us to have a desire for the things of God and then He leads us and teaches us how to fulfill these desires. Some gifts will be easier to operate in because of your personality, motivational, and/or five-fold gifting. These gifts usually have a tangible anointing that will accompany them. You may feel as if you are getting warm all over, as if your breath has instantly become shortened, or you may even feel overwhelmed by the Holy Spirit. To some, this feels like an anxiety attack. It is the Holy Spirit getting your attention so that He can show what He desires to do through you. Once you realize what is happening, clarity will come to you concerning a need or circumstance, along with the understanding that you are to address. Many of these gifts will be very natural for you to operate in and will occur easily. Another way to recognize these gifts is by analyzing what is happening while you are under the anointing. What is your first thought? Is it to find someone to pray for or is it to prophesy? This will reveal your heart's desire.

OPERATION:

You must always regard the etiquette of the church when operating within the local church setting. Look for the opportune time to release the word, tongue, or interpretation (for instance, in between songs, or at a quiet point in the service). Look for openness and faith on the part of the receiver for individual words. Never bombard or overwhelm someone who is not ready to receive. Prophecy will be revelation of an event or need, with a promise from God to get involved. It will be edifying, exhorting, and comforting. It can deal with the past, present, or future. There is never condemnation in God's words, but always reveal the love of God. Tongues and interpretation will operate in these same realms. The Holy Spirit is the initiator of these gifts; it is called the unction. These three gifts will never operate without His unction, except for when we speak the sure word of prophecy (scripture), which is already inspired and can be initiated by prayer. This is a safe way to step out in faith. If you receive a word and are a little intimidated to give it verbally, write it down and give it to them. This is better than doing nothing. Although the word should be uttered, this is still effective. Ask God to use you in these three gifts and prepare yourself to jump in and make a difference in someone's life.

DEVELOPMENT:

An intimate relationship with the Lord is the key to developing the gifts of utterance, because you must know the person on whose behalf you are speaking. You have His heart and intention in mind. Prayer develops this intimacy; reading develops godly personality and accuracy. Obedience is the key to God trusting you and being able to use you whenever He desires. Through obedience, you will be used of God, and your gift will increase by the reason of your use. The more you give, the more you receive. Challenge yourself and be willing to fail sometimes. Mistakes will not end your ability to be used or God's desire to use you. Humbly accept your mistake and move on. Ask the Holy Spirit to teach and lead you, and you'll be okay. Pray, read, and obey, and your life will change for the better.

CHAPTER 17

THE FINAL CALL

The Supernatural Church

> "The glory of this latter temple shall be greater than the former," says the LORD of hosts. "And in this place I will give peace," says the LORD of hosts.

Haggai 2:9, NKJV

WHO IS CALLED TO BE A "SUPERNATURALIST"?

All are called to be supernaturalists, meaning, all are called to be led by the Holy Spirit and rely on the spiritual gifts of the Spirit of God. Joseph was brought before Pharaoh and this generation will stand before great men by the use of their spiritual gifts.

Politicians will give prophetic words behind closed doors to other politicians. Fashion models, in the changing room, will be praying for other models that need a touch from God. In all walks of life, the Holy Spirit will be able to use us at any time He desires.

Why is this so difficult for us to believe? The psychic hotline brought in over two billion dollars a year at its peak. The leading television shows consist of subjects such as aliens and paranormal events. The devil is trying to distract and confuse people from Kingdom business. Consequently, this is all working for the good of the furthering of the gospel; it is just stirring interest and desire for true supernatural power. The demand for spiritual equipping is rising in the world and the church. Let the true leaders of the world get in front of the next move that is going to hit this planet. Already, corporations are organizing seminars and conventions for eastern meditation, hypnotism, and occult activities. These same corporations are calling in psychics to give spiritual guidance for future business dealings. At the time of this writing, our government has spent twenty million dollars over the last twenty years on psychic advice. That's one million dollars a year. This money could be going to missionary work if we would get our act together and believe God to give us the gifts that the world is desiring to find. We must be bold enough to meet the need of this spiritually bankrupt society. We are entrusted by God to touch this generation for such a time as this! It is incredible how God believes and trusts in us, so much so that He has saved us for this space of time.

The mandate is set, the gifts are given, and the land is ours to possess. Our marching orders read, "Soldiers of redemption, possess and occupy all territories!" The objective of a soldier of redemption is to redeem the time, redeem souls, and everything that the devil has tried to keep from us. All things that have been lost, stolen, or blinded from our eyes. Take it back; for you are equipped to do so!

A soldier of redemption is a supernaturalist and must be acquainted with the three Ps of Possessing: Pressure, Passion, and Power.

PRESSURE

Supernaturalists are people who know how to adjust to pressure. As a Christian, there are many pressures that come with the lifestyle. Pressures of life, pressures of persecution, pressures of living godly, pressures of spiritual attacks and testing, and pressures of faithfulness. Just as a diamond is formed by pressure, these pressures form us into a precious gem for the Kingdom of God. We, as supernaturalists, will learn to appreciate these seasons of pressure, knowing that momentary affliction cannot be compared with the glory that shall be revealed in us.

Deep-sea divers rely on the engineer of the ship on the surface of the ocean. As the diver descends into the deep, dark abyss, he must be careful to have a light to see and pressure meters available. The light is to illuminate his way when he gets too deep to see what is in front of him. The deeper he goes, the darker it will become. The engineer in the ship above must regulate the pressure of the diving suit according to the pressure that is coming against the diver the deeper he goes. If, for whatever reason, his suit fails to adjust to this precise pressure, it would cause the diver to implode. The inward pressure must be the same or more as the outward pressure.

Each day, there are people who go through this implosion in the form of suicide, nervous breakdowns, mental illness, depression, and oppression. These are just a few ways that implosion manifests in lives when people don't know how to adjust to the pressures of life. Spiritual deficiencies cause emotional and physical breakdown.

Being supernatural is not acting like weirdo freaks that always seem as if they are living on cloud nine. Being supernatural is learning how to apply the mind of Christ in every environment of life, imparting instead of drawing, and walking in the power of the resurrected King in every opportunity. As supernatural people go through pressures, they find a light in the time of darkness. Looking in the Word, waiting for the word of the Lord, knowing that as soon as the word comes, faith rises and doubt flees, angels come and the devil leaves. The Word brings illumination. David exclaimed that the entrance of God's Word brings light and understanding. This is what the devil hates; men and women of God who trust in the Word of the Lord. God's light will illuminate any abyss we find ourselves in.

Each time I have gone through a trial, I found peace in the Word of God and held onto any scripture that would fit my circumstances. I felt that, at any time, I could sink if I let go of His Word, but as long as I held on, I would be okay. With every one of these trials, I heard the voice of God right before the trial was finished. As soon as I heard His voice, I held onto the written and the spoken Word. The devil was in trouble! When you have both the written Word and the Spirit working, your soul will be anchored in the Word of the Lord and the enemy can't blind you any longer.

Fortunately, the engineer in our ships of life is our diving buddy and knows what is going on in our lives and can encourage us as we walk. There is no better prayer partner than the Holy Spirit. When we don't feel like praying, or if we don't know how to pray, He prays with and for us. As we pray in the Spirit, we build up our most holy faith, building our spirit-man within these diving suits so that we can withstand the pressures of life. When you find yourself under pressure, you should find yourself praying in the Spirit even more than usual. This will result in your inward strength to balance the outward pressure. The enemy hates this as well, because instead of having a hissy fit at the times that you would normally lose your cool, you walk through with faith that cannot be moved, overcoming all doubt, fear, and unbelief!

PASSION

This faith will result in vision and vision will result in passion. Every person has some type of passion, but of course, not all passion is progressive. A person can find their passion through analyzing what makes them tick or what makes them ticked. Passion is an emotion that fuels action toward a set vision. Anger, fear, frustration, lust, pride, and love are all forms of passion. Each one of these emotions forms an outlook on a vision. Young people in the ghetto find themselves forming a vision of escaping the bondage of poverty and lack because of the anger that has been formed from not having what they need. Children from broken families make up their minds that they will do whatever it takes to have a good and healthy marriage. These passions are formed through hardships, but they can still create progressive passions for transformation instead of conforming. Supernaturalists will learn to take the difficulties and disappointments of pressure and turn them into progressive passion. Once the passion is in play, then the person of passion will be consumed with ideas of making these visions come to pass. First comes pressure, then vision, faith and hope, and finally action, keeping passion progressive instead of destructive. Hitler had passion, but his passion didn't care about who he walked over or hurt. His passion was ungodly and not for the betterment of mankind or the Kingdom of God. The whole idea is that men and women of God must have a passion that will make them willing to do whatever it takes to further the Kingdom of God.

The prophetic ministry is here to help us harness our passion to the highest productivity. If a person has vision and passion toward their purpose, they will go through every obstacle and jump any hurdle to reach that goal. The word of the Lord is like the finish line to a hurdler. A hurdler doesn't focus on the hurdles that are in front of him, his eyes are always on the string at the finish line. Actually, an accomplished hurdler will know exactly how many steps there are between each hurdle, so that he will never have to look anywhere other than the finish line. Supernatural people will not have to worry about the steps to the vision because they know that their steps are ordered by the Lord. They are already set! Keep godly passion and know that the Lord has everything else taken care of.

POWER

The Lord has never given anyone a purpose and then withheld the power needed to accomplish what was set before him or her. We are empowered to fulfill the vision that is set before us. We are getting close to the end, and the closer we get, the greater the fight is. But the truth of the matter is that this generation will never be happy unless they are fighting. No other generation has ever had to go through what this generation is called to go through. On the other hand, there has never been a generation that has been so empowered like this generation. We are empowered technologically and intellectually; more equipped than any other people to take this world.

The Lord has saved the best for last and empowered us for this last day! This is the reason many of us are so dissatisfied; we have a sense of greatness but don't understand it. We tend to blame this dissatisfaction on our jobs, marriages, families, or lack of material gain. The truth is that these frustrations are from a divine dissatisfaction upon a warring generation. Warriors are not happy unless they are at war. Joshua's generation was formed for war. Their purpose was to take the children of God into the Promised Land, overcoming the enemies that possessed the land. Just as they were empowered to possess, so are we empowered to possess!

Prepare to take possession of your promise!

GIFTS TEST

1. **WHICH OF THE FOLLOWING ARE YOUR STRONGEST TWO DESIRES?**

   - ☐ a. Help people who are hurting.
   - ☐ b. Have understanding.
   - ☐ c. Know the details of circumstances.
   - ☐ d. Believe for the impossible.
   - ☐ e. Give people answers and understanding.
   - ☐ f. Give instruction on how to solve problems.
   - ☐ g. Ability to supernaturally communicate God's Word in foreign languages.
   - ☐ h. Ability to breakdown communication problems.
   - ☐ i. Follow instructions that will create a dramatic change.

2. **IF YOU SEE A YOUNG MAN/WOMAN SITTING ON THE SIDE OF THE ROAD, WITH THEIR FACE IN THEIR HANDS AS IF THEY WERE IN NEED, WHAT WOULD BE YOUR FIRST THOUGHT?**

   - ☐ a. They must be in pain; spiritually, emotionally, or physically.
   - ☐ b. I wonder what the circumstances are in their life?
   - ☐ c. I wonder what God has to say to this young man/woman?

3. **IF YOU HAVE A CHANCE TO MINISTER TO HIM/ HER, WHAT WOULD YOU DO?**

☐ a. Ask if he/she needed prayer or if you could pray for him/her.
☐ b. Sit next to him/her and begin communication, waiting for an opportunity to minister.
☐ c. Intercede from a distance, then approach him/her when you're sure of what to do.
☐ d. Walk on.

4. **WHAT IS MOST IMPORTANT TO YOU?**

☐ a. Hearing from God.
☐ b. Seeing God's power.
☐ c. Speaking on God's behalf.

5. **BASED UPON THE DEFINITIONS OF THE GIFTS OF THE SPIRIT IN THIS BOOK, WHICH OF THE FOLLOWING TWO GIFTS DO YOU FIND MOST LIFE-CHANGING?**

☐ a. Gifts of healings
☐ b. Gift of prophecy
☐ c. Gift of the word of knowledge
☐ d. Gift of discerning of spirits
☐ e. Gift of word of wisdom
☐ f. Gift of tongues
☐ g. Gift of interpretation
☐ h. Gift of faith
☐ i. Gift of working of miracles

NOTES